PRAISE FOR THE POCKET

"Jason Boyett's Pocket Guides are smart and hilarious. And they're sneaky too. You don't realize how much you're learning because you're having so much fun."
—AJ Jacobs, author, *The Year of Living Biblically*

"Hewing to his
Stewart model, J
collection of Po
not careful, you
with a curiosity
wry irreverence—
delightful volumes." —Lauren Sandler, author, *Righteous: Dispatches from the Evangelical Youth Movement*

"Boyett's witty, weird and sometimes even wise Pocket Guides are proof that the best things do come in small packages
you real
—Danie
Parallel U

"Irrevere
more 21
the Qur'
Pocket G
the annoy
club." —
and The S

"The Pocket Guides are more fun than a plague of frogs, more satisfying than manna from heaven and way less expensive than attending seminary. Pocket Guide to the Bible, to Sainthood and to the Afterlife achieve the remarkable feat of being absurdly funny, surprisingly full of legitimate Biblical information and, inexplicably, provoking a deeper understanding of my faith. Jason Boyett is a truly inspired and disturbed individual and for that I am grateful." —Dan Merchant, writer/producer/director of *Lord, Save Us from Your Followers*

"Here's a writer with insight like a finger in the eye, but you later want to thank him for that finger in the eye. If there were a Pocket Guide to Jason Boyett, it would include words like Fearless, Deep, and Snarky. And did I mention funny? Oh my goodness this guy is funny." —Dean Nelson, author, *God Hides in Plain Sight,* and director, Writer's Symposium by the Sea at Point Loma

Other Books by Jason Boyett

Pocket Guide to the Bible

Pocket Guide to Sainthood

Pocket Guide to the Apocalypse

POCKET GUIDE

TO THE

AFTERLIFE

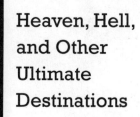

Heaven, Hell,
and Other
Ultimate
Destinations

Jason Boyett

JOSSEY-BASS
A Wiley Imprint
www.josseybass.com

Library of Congress Cataloging-in-Publication Data

Boyett, Jason.
    Pocket guide to the afterlife : heaven, hell, and other ultimate destinations / Jason Boyett.
      p. cm.
    Includes bibliographical references (p.   ).
    ISBN 978-0-470-37311-8 (pbk.)
    1. Future life. I. Title.
  BL535.B69 2009
  202'.3—dc22   2009013919

Printed in the United States of America
FIRST EDITION
PB Printing   10 9 8 7 6 5 4 3 2 1

CONTENTS

INTRODUCTION

William Winchester died of tuberculosis in 1881. He was rich and famous, the son of Oliver Winchester, whose company developed the Winchester Rifle and made a fortune during the Civil War and expansion of the American West. But he still died. William left his wife, Sarah, an inheritance of $20 million and an additional $1,000 a day in gun royalties. Despite the cash, Sarah was devastated. If by "devastated" you mean "transformed from Sarah Winchester, the Connecticut socialite, into Old Widow Winchester, the nuttiest nutball on the West Coast."

Spiritualism had become a big deal during the late nineteenth century, especially among the wealthy elite. So a friend suggested, after William's death, that Sarah check in with a local medium. The medium could maybe talk to William and somehow ease Sarah's pain. It was a great plan, until the medium (allegedly) reached out and touched the eternal void. William wasn't available, but the word on Afterlife Boulevard was bad. *Real* bad. Apparently, the Winchester family was cursed by the vengeful ghosts of everyone who'd ever died at the end of a Winchester rifle. And considering that Winchester sold thousands of rifles to the U.S. government during the Civil War, that was a lot of vengeful ghosts. Thousands. Probably tens of thousands. Furthermore, the medium revealed that the only way to keep these armies of avenging spirits under control was for Sarah to move West and start building a house. And if she ever stopped building the house? The ghosts would show up and drag Sarah, kicking and screaming, into eternity.

Crap.

Sarah, being completely psycho at this point, thought the medium's message sounded sensible enough. And being human, she didn't want to die. So she moved to California, bought an 8-room farmhouse on 162 acres in San Jose, hired a construction crew, and went crazy. For the rest of her life, Sarah used her fortune to make additions to the house. She kept the crews busy 24 hours a day, 7 days a week, 365 days a year. It never stopped. The house ended up with 40 bedrooms, 10,000 windows, 2,000 doors, fireplaces without chimneys, and staircases that led nowhere. Sarah designed it all.

The work continued for thirty-eight insane years until Sarah died in her sleep in 1922. She was eighty-five. Construction stopped immediately, leaving a sweet tourist destination—the Winchester Mystery House[1]—for the city of San Jose, and one awesome story for the rest of us. It's a story about a lady who went to a lot of trouble while alive because she was obsessed with death. Her fear

---

1. It's open daily for guided tours. See www.winchestermysteryhouse.com.

and fascination with what she'd encounter on the other side of the cosmic curtain drove her to Wackytown.

Few of us turn to demented construction in order to stave off death, but at the end of the day, most of us are a little like Sarah. We spend a lot of time thinking about what happens once we draw our last breath.

We contemplate death while buying life insurance policies. We frown at it during newscasts. We're even entertained by it, since pretty much every television drama for the past three decades has been about forensic investigators, homicide detectives, murderers, trial lawyers, hospitals, ghosts, vampire slayers, and/or people presumed to be dead but living on a mysterious island. We're well acquainted with mortality. Probably too much.

But what we're not so sure about is what happens on the back end of this mortal coil. Other than a few random heart-attack patients and/or best-selling authors, very few of us have been to the other side and returned to tell about it. The whole thing's a locked box behind a secret wall within the hidden basement of a crazy lady's mystery house.

Thankfully, we have religious traditions to shed gauzy, soft-focus light on the Great Beyond. And most of them—from Aztec mythology to Zoroastrianism, from the ancient Egyptians to contemporary Mormons—have some notion that death isn't the end. Something else happens once the closing credits roll. But these traditions can't agree on what exactly that something is. Or where it takes place. Or how long it will last. Or whether or not a demon will be present there to devour our soul.[2]

But as long as our individual death rate keeps hovering around the 100 percent mark, the afterlife is gonna be of interest to us. Which means you, dear reader, should be knowledgeable about it. That's where the *Pocket Guide* comes in. Consider it your personal tour guide to the everlasting unknown. You'll learn how to talk about the afterlife like a reasonable, completely not-crazy person. You'll learn what people have thought, taught, and written about it for the past few thousand years. You'll learn your possible destination (Heaven? Hell? The Chinvat Bridge?) and what you might expect there. You'll also learn how to pronounce Mictlantecuhtli, the name of the Aztec god of death.[3]

Clearly you need to read this book—if not for this life, then for the next. Pull up a chair, take a deep breath, and let's ponder our eventual demise. It'll be great!

---

2. If the prospect of this happening concerns you, turn right this minute to the entry on Duat on p. 103 in Chapter 4.

3. But you'll have to read all the way through to Chapter 7. Can't wait? It's on p. 176.

CHAPTER 1

The Cosmic Lexicon
(A Glossary of the Hereafter)

When it comes to the afterlife, there is one, and only one, place to start: religion. Albert Einstein once said that the essence of religion was humanity's attempt to understand mystery. Because the afterlife is a mysterious topic—and because the *Pocket Guide* always chooses to trust Einstein for reasons of him being a genius—it makes sense for our religious traditions to try to figure out what happens after we die. This is helpful, but there are a lot of religions. A *lot*. And while it's nice that they've spent the last few millennia trying to solve the same big afterlifey questions, none of their answers agree upon much.

Which means navigating their theories can be tricky. Christians are big on **salvation** but look confused when you ask them about **moksha.** Muslims can talk for hours about the **Five Pillars** but could care less about the **Eightfold Path.** Westerners are familiar with terms such as **reincarnation** and **karma**, but don't know if they're Buddhist concepts or Hindu beliefs or just something they heard about from that hot chick at the gym.

That's what happens with a broad, weird, complicated subject like the afterlife. It creates a vocabulary all its own. It's rich with pious phrases (**born again**), egghead terminology (**metempsychosis**), words you can't pronounce (**chthonic**), and activities in which you probably shouldn't participate (**necromancy**).

Don't worry, though. The *Pocket Guide* is here to serve. Before we dig too deep into the afterlife—clever cemetery-themed play on words, no?—let's start with a glossary. These are the words and concepts you need to know before emancipating your soul, atoning for your sins, or otherwise continuing in this book. Tune up your harps, kids. It's time for fun with **thanatology**!

🌺 ANGEL

A heavenly being. In Jewish and Christian traditions, angels are often tasked with interacting with mankind on God's behalf. In the Bible, angels do cool things like rescuing Lot from the about-to-be-annihilated Sodom, telling Mary she's pregnant with Jesus, and performing a covert prison extraction on behalf of a locked-up Peter.[1]

The angels of Islam are even more impressive, carrying out the killer tasks no one else really wants to do. According to the Qu'ran, specific angels are responsible for keeping track of the daily good and bad deeds of every human, making sure it rains, and guarding the gates of hell. Islamic angels aren't just bookkeepers or sentries, though. A whole squadron of them—nineteen not-to-be-messed-

---

1. Genesis 19:1, Exodus 33:2, Luke 1:26, Acts 5:19 (respectively). Unless otherwise noted, all scriptural citations are from the New International Version of the Bible.

with "wardens of the fire"—are responsible for actively punishing souls in hell.[2] It should be noted that these angels rarely show up as porcelain collectibles.

Please use it in a sentence or two: Seeing how angels are always telling Bible characters not to be afraid of them, one must assume angels aren't adorable little apple-cheeked, curly-haired babies. No, they're *scary* little apple-cheeked babies.

Not to be confused with: Anything sporting a halo and appearing on cutesy home decorations, calendars, key chains, and/or teacups.

❀ ANNIHILATIONISM

The belief, held by a minority of Christians, that immortality is granted only to inhabitants of heaven. The unredeemed who go to hell aren't tortured forever and ever. They're just destroyed. *Poof.* That's their everlasting punishment: nonexistence.

Some annihilationists believe that sinners will literally be consumed by hellfire until they disappear into the bubbling magma. So there's a little bit of torment involved, but it ends quickly. Other annihilationists don't believe in hell at all.

Please use it in a sentence or two: Christians who believe in annihilationism have a hard time with the idea of a loving God who infinitely torments sinners for committing a finite number of sins. The rest of the Christians think annihilationists are probably bound for hell.

Not to be confused with: *Ucchedavada,* the generally frowned-upon belief in post-death annihilation held by a few rebel Buddhists.

---

2. Qur'an 74:31.

❧ APOCALYPSE

The devastating, end-of-the-world event—resulting from super-natural intervention, natural disaster, or something humanity did (oops!)—that results in the complete destruction of life on earth. Or the entire universe, depending on the scope of the event.

Within the Christian faith, you'll occasionally hear the word used in conjunction with the Second Coming of Christ or as a synonym for the New Testament book of Revelation. Which makes sense, because *apocalypse* comes from the Greek word *apokalypsis,* which means "the lifting of a veil"—a revelation.

Please use it in a sentence: I believe the apocalypse will result either from an out-of-control asteroid, a nuclear holocaust, or the ironic combination of the two should the Air Force use an intercontinental ballistic missile to shoot down a wayward asteroid but miss their target, much to the dismay of Western Europe.

Not to be confused with: *Apocalypto,* the 2006 Mel Gibson movie about the demise of the Mayan civilization. This film caused dismay in Western Europe, but for other reasons.

❧ ATMAN

The vital force or true self, as identified by **Hinduism** and **Jainism**. And FYI, it's pronounced "ott-MAHN." As opposed to any pronunciation that rhymes with *Batman*.

See also: *Soul*.

❧ BARDO THODOL

See *Book of the Dead,* Tibetan.

❧ *BOOK OF THE DEAD,* EGYPTIAN

An illustrated papyrus scroll frequently found in Egyptian tombs or coffins, used to guide a deceased Egyptian through the afterlife and into the blissful Aaru, the Field of Reeds. The main purpose of these scrolls—which were traditionally placed within reach of the deceased—was to keep the newly dead person from getting lost in the perilous underworld. All manner of navigational clues, passwords, songs, magical incantations (like the **Negative Confession**), and other handy tips were contained within the scroll.

Because there's a great deal of variance from one book of the dead to another, it is assumed that wealthy Egyptians arranged for customized books to be created prior to their deaths. Middle-class folks got stuck with a boilerplate book, with their pictographic names hastily scribbled into *insert-name-here* blanks.

The Egyptians didn't call it "the *Egyptian Book of the Dead,*" by the way; their title was *Going Forth by Day.*

Please use it in a sentence: Darlene caused quite a scene at the funeral home when she got caught stuffing a large papyrus scroll into Grandfather's coffin, claiming he needed it to remember all the parts of the Negative Confession, especially since he always got stuck on "I haven't carried away the khenfu cakes from the Spirits of the dead."[3]

Not to be confused with: The *Tibetan Book of the Dead,* which has fewer pictures but lots more monsters.

---

3. From the *Papyrus of Ani,* history's most famous Egyptian *Book of the Dead. The Book of the Dead: Papyrus of Ani,* E. A. Wallis Budge, trans. (Sioux Falls, SD: NuVision Publications, 2009), p. 90.

🌻 *BOOK OF THE DEAD,* TIBETAN

A Buddhist text describing in outrageous detail what happens during the period (called *bardo*) between death and reincarnation. Supposedly written in the eighth century and known as the *Bardo Thodol,* it wasn't translated into English until the twentieth century, but *boy* is the *Pocket Guide* glad the thing eventually made its way West.

Its best-known chapter—"The Great Liberation by Hearing"—is intended to direct a recently dead person as he or she encounters one horrifying deity after another on the way to rebirth. These include the demonic "Gauri of the eastern direction," who stands "wrathful, white, and aloof" on no less than a throne of human carcasses, all while swinging around a single corpse like a gory, gangly baseball bat.[4] Also worth mentioning: "Padma Heruka, who has three faces / Dark red, white, and blue; and six arms,"[5] and "black bear-headed Indrani," who holds a "noose of entrails,"[6] which seems too slippery to be effective as a weapon, but who is the *Pocket Guide* to argue with a bear-headed demon?

Anyway, occasionally a *lama* will recite the *Bardo Thodol* to a dead person to make sure they know what to do should they encounter any six-armed, corpse-swinging demons on the way to the next life.

Please use it in a sentence: Don't read the *Tibetan Book of the Dead* late at night, as it will scare the deer-headed Siddhikari right out of you.[7]

---

4. Padmasambhava. *The Tibetan Book of the Dead,* Graham Coleman, Gyurme Dorje, Thupten Jinpa, eds. (New York: Viking Penguin, 2006), p. 105.

5. Ibid., 104.

6. Ibid., 110.

7. Ibid., 111.

Not to be confused with: The *Egyptian Book of the Dead,* which has a lot more singing and fewer skullcaps filled with blood.

 BORN AGAIN

A synonym used by some adherents of Protestant Christianity to refer to the process of **salvation,** based on Jesus' statement to Nicodemus in John 3:3—"I tell you the truth, no one can see the kingdom of God unless he is born again." Conservative Christians tend to view a "born again" experience as a prerequisite for entrance into heaven.

Please use it in a sentence or two: Jose said he was born again as a child when he responded to an altar call at a Billy Graham crusade. Then he was born again at a Christian youth camp in eighth grade. And he was born again once more at a True Love Waits rally when he was seventeen. Jose was always an overachiever.

Not to be confused with: Jose's experience.

9

❧ BUDDHISM

A religion that developed out of Hinduism and is based on the teachings of Guatama Buddha. The Buddha experienced enlightenment somewhere around the fourth or fifth century B.C.E., once he determined that—contrary to Hindu beliefs—there was no such thing as the **atman**, or soul. He also realized that life involves a lot of suffering, which he defined as being too attached to the transience of the world.[8] But suffering can be alleviated by following the **Four Noble Truths** and adhering to the **Eightfold Path** and eventually attaining a state of self-purification and understanding called **moksha**, or liberation from the cycle of rebirth or **reincarnation.**

Buddhism began in India but has since lost ground there and spread into Cambodia, China, Japan, Korea, Laos, Myanmar/Burma, Sri Lanka, Thailand, Tibet, and the Hollywood Hills. An estimated 350–400 million adherents make it the fourth largest religion in the world, behind Christianity, Islam, and Hinduism.

Buddhists you've probably heard of: Orlando Bloom, Richard Gere, Keanu Reeves, Steven Seagal, Uma Thurman, Adam Yauch of the Beastie Boys, and the Dalai Lama.

❧ CHRISTIANITY

With some 2 billion adherents, it's the world's largest religion and the one you probably default to when you think about the afterlife. Christianity grew out of Judaism in the first century A.D. (a calendar distinction related to Christ's birth, by the way) and has its

---

8. A decent theory, but don't use this line to comfort someone at a funeral. "Quit crying! You're just too attached to the transience of this world, anyway."

origins in the life, death, resurrection, and teachings of Jesus. Christians believe Jesus to be the Son of God, through whom people are reconciled to God, and through whom their sins may be forgiven.

After his death and resurrection, Jesus ascended into the sky—so, obviously, heaven is up *there* somewhere—but will eventually return in the Second Coming, an event tied to notions of the **apocalypse**. Despite a few major doctrinal conflicts among the three main branches of Christianity (Catholic, Protestant, and Orthodox), most believe forgiven followers of Christ will be rewarded with life in heaven after they die, where they will enjoy a blissful eternity in the presence of God. Nonbelievers who die in their sin are cast out of the presence of God and into hell, where they can expect to become familiar with the "gnashing of teeth."[9]

Christians you've probably heard of: Pope Benedict XVI, Bono, Billy Graham, Barack Obama, Joel Osteen, Rick Warren.

❧ CHTHONIC

In Greek mythology, the term used to describe the gods of the underworld—like Hades and Persephone[10]—as opposed to the regular Olympian gods like Zeus and Aphrodite. The "underworld" encompassed the final resting place of both the virtuous dead (who end up in the Elysian Fields) and the less-than-virtuous dead (destination: Tartarus).

And it's pronounced "THON-ic," as most dictionaries make the "ch" silent. Except for the pretentious *Oxford English Dictionary,*

---

9. An excellent phrase in the King James Version of the Bible, appearing six times in the Gospel of Matthew and once in the Gospel of Luke, always related to the final destination of the wicked.

10. Respectively, the god of the dead and queen of the underworld.

which feels this is just the Americans being lazy about pronunciation and insists you say "kuh-THON-ic."

Please use it in a sentence: *You* use it in a sentence. The *Pocket Guide* is still working on the pronunciation.

Not to be confused with: *Chthonic,* the melodic black metal band from Taiwan, who paint their faces into ghoulish Gene Simmons–like death masks but who are not, in fact, the kings and queens of hell. Unless you consider OzzFest to be a surrogate for hell.

❧ CREMATION

The practice of incinerating the soft parts of a dead body as an alternative to the traditional casket-and-burial route. Cremation is central to **Hinduism**, whose adherents believe it's the first step in the process of **reincarnation.** It's less popular among Christians, who tend to worry what kinds of bodies they'll have at the resurrection if their only remains have been flung willy-nilly into a garden somewhere, or, worse, sprinkled into a mountain stream. Islam, Zoroastrianism, and Orthodox Judaism forbid cremation outright.[11]

Please use it in a sentence: Doug chose cremation for the same reasons most people do—because it's dignified, it's economical, it's environmentally sound, and because he'd always been something of a pyro.

❧ DAMNATION

What happens to unsaved sinners after they die, according to the teachings of Christianity. Damnation is bad on all fronts because it

---

11. Jewish law states that the soul of a cremated person is unable to reach a final place of rest . . . which made the Nazi-operated crematoriums during the Holocaust even more of an atrocity.

involves not just the condemnation to hell but also the denial of entrance to heaven.

Please use it in a sentence or two: Carlos used to laugh whenever that street preacher yelled at him about eternal damnation. But now that he was stuck in hell, chained naked to a flaming cactus while being perpetually pepper-sprayed in both eyes by a winged demon, he figured he might have been too quick to judge.

Not to be confused with: *Tarnation,* the cartoonish, colloquial synonym for damnation made popular by Yosemite Sam.

✹ DEMON

An evil spirit in the Christian, Jewish, Islamic, and Hindu religious traditions, as well as in comic books (*Etrigan*), cult television programs (*Buffy the Vampire Slayer*), and movies starring Ron Perlman (*Hellboy*). Popular theology makes demons into the whip-cracking taskmasters of hell, but this isn't exactly supported by the Bible (where demons possess people but do little else) or the teachings of Islam (where "creatures of fire" called jinns may be good or evil and often look like cats) or Hindu mythology (where demons are *really* scary and may be flesh-eating *pishacha*s, or vampirish *vetala*s who make their homes in corpses, or shape-shifting cannibalistic *rakshasa*s). Nevertheless, each tradition places demons within a detailed hierarchy, and it's generally understood that you don't want to meet up with one, in this life or the next.

Please use it in a sentence or two: Keep your hands off that ouija board, kids. It's possessed by demons (*Christian version*).

Keep your hands off that ouija board, kids. It's possessed by a *rakshasa* who wants to devour your face (*Hindu version*).

Not to be confused with: That shiny horned beast in the Tenacious D song "Tribute," who forces the boys to either play the best song in the world or have their souls eaten. Demons are just not that interested in comedic rock opera.

🌿 EIGHTFOLD PATH

A traditional Buddhist teaching that gives eight practical tips to transcend suffering via the pursuit of nirvana. These tips or principles fall into three categories: *Wisdom* (right view, right intention); *Ethical Conduct* (right speech, right action, right livelihood); and *Mental Development* (right effort, right mindfulness, right concentration). Get all of these, uh, right and not only will you end suffering, but you'll reach a higher level of existence in the next life. And maybe the one after that. Right on.

Not to be confused with: *The Eight Immortals,* legendary figures in Chinese mythology who lived on the mystical Penglai Mountain-Island and had individual powers, just like the Superfriends but without the tights and capes.

🌿 EMBALMING

The practice of chemically preserving a corpse after death in order to minimize decay. While embalming is still used today to prepare human remains for presentation, it first became popular in ancient Egyptian culture. The Egyptians combined embalming with mummification, believing the body to be the eternal night-time refueling station of a person's soul (known as the *Ba*), after it had gone forth into the afterlife during the day-time. Without an embalmed body, the *Ba* would be damned to rootless roving around in the afterlife, like some of those hipster backpacker kids in South Asia, only not as scary.

Please use it in a sentence: Most people don't like to think about embalming, probably because of those nasty stories about how the ancient Egyptians extracted a corpse's brains using hooks inserted through the nose.

Not to be confused with: *Taxidermy,* which involves preserving animals shot by hunters. If there's any "going forth by day" of these animals' souls, then those hunting lodges filled with stuffed-and-mounted elk heads and bear skins are horrifying places indeed.

ESCHATOLOGY

The branch of theology concerned with the end of the world, the final destiny of humanity, the **apocalypse**, and other cheery topics. Almost every world religion—from the ancient Aztecs to Zoro-astrianism—has something to say about the End Times. It's rarely encouraging.

Please use it in a sentence: Remember when Gerard got all into eschatology and started sending us those e-mails identifying Oprah as the Antichrist?

Not to be confused with: *Thanatology,* the academic study of death, usually as it relates to individuals. Eschatology is to thanatology what thermonuclear detonation is to a 4th of July sparkler.

ETERNAL LIFE

The unending existence awaiting humanity, based on the belief that physical death is only one stop on a really long bus ride that continues for pretty much ever. In **Christianity,** eternal life comes through salvation offered by the death and resurrection of Jesus Christ. In **Islam,** eternal life is often described as a "blissful here-after," earned by performing good deeds and adhering to the **Five Pillars of Islam.** In cyclical religions like Buddhism, eternal life is implied by **reincarnation** from one life to another, depending on the quality of your **karma.**

15

Nevertheless, most religions promise an encore to your present life by way of an everlasting future. Hopefully, this future comes equipped with a full schedule of activities and a Netflix subscription, because eternity can be a loooooong time.

Please use it in a sentence: Before he died, Granddad insisted that we hide his baseball glove, sand wedge, and a few range balls in his casket, fearing he'd run out of ways to pass the time during his eternal life.

Not to be confused with: *Eternal Fire,* a punishment prepared for the "devil and his angels" and awaiting those who fail to attend to the needy, as threatened by Jesus in Matthew 25:41.[12] While you're at it, don't confuse *Eternal Fire* with "Eternal Flame," a tormenting mid-'80s song by the Bangles.

❧ FIVE PILLARS OF ISLAM

The five fundamental obligations every good Muslim must follow in the pursuit of **eternal life.**[13] The first is the *Shahada,* the creedal profession of faith ("There is no God but Allah."). The second one is *Salat,* the compulsory prayers offered five times a day. The third is *Zakat,* charitable giving toward the needy. The fourth is *Hajj,* a pilgrimage to Mecca at least once before death by every able-bodied Muslim. And the fifth is *Sawm,* the ritual fast during the month of Ramadan.

Please use it in a sentence: If the National Football League ever expanded into a Muslim nation and one of the resulting teams

---

12. "Eternal fire" is also promised, in Jude 1:7, to towns like Sodom and Gomorrah who "gave themselves up to sexual immorality and perversion." So watch out.

13. Only the majority Sunni Muslims observe the official Five Pillars. Minority Shi'a Muslims list up to ten practices they must perform. There may be fewer Shi'a numerically, but they're twice as holy as the Sunnis.

had an especially ferocious offensive line, they would totally be nicknamed the "Five Pillars of Islam."

Not to be confused with: The mythological *Five Pillows of Islam,* thought to exist in the ancient bedchamber of a legendary imam, probably lost to the scouring desert sands of the Middle East, and possibly the result of a mistranslation anyway.

❧ FOUR NOBLE TRUTHS

A fundamental teaching in Buddhism, based on what Guatama Buddha learned when he got all enlightened. The gist of his transcendental education can be summed up by four distinct truths. One: There is such a thing as suffering. Two: Suffering has a cause (attachment to silly transitory notions like "the world" or "the self" or "chocolate"). Three: Suffering can eventually be stopped, suppressed, or otherwise escaped from, via enlightenment. Four: Enlightenment can be achieved by way of the Eightfold Path.

So it's a little misleading, because while there are only four truths, the last one is an eight-parter.

Not to be confused with: The *Five Pillars of Islam,* the *Three Persons of the Trinity,* or the *Oceanic Six*.

❧ GHOST

The disembodied spirit of a dead person, often thought to be a visible manifestation of the soul, which may or may not resemble Hamlet's father, the Stay-Puft Marshmallow Man, or (spoiler alert!) Bruce Willis. Ghosts and ghost stories appear in almost every culture and religious tradition and represent the idea that the soul is distinctly separate from the body and able to exist in some fashion even after the physical body is gone. Yep: **eternal life.**

There are lots of theories about ghosts, but one of the most popular ones suggests a ghost has unfinished business on earth and, as a result, exists in some netherworld between the living and the dead.

Most people don't believe in ghosts, but the biblical writers did. According to 1 Samuel 28, King Saul used a medium to put him in touch with the dead prophet Samuel, who ends up "coming up out of the ground" (NIV) and scolding Saul for disturbing his eternal rest.

Please use it in a sentence: Sharon used to believe in ghosts, until Scooby-Doo ruined them for her forever.

Not to be confused with: *The Holy Ghost,* an old-fashioned name for the third person of the Christian Trinity, also known as the Holy Spirit. The Holy Ghost is usually represented by a white dove. As opposed to a white bed sheet.

❦ HARROWING OF HELL

The Christian doctrine, mentioned in the "He descended into hell" part of the Apostle's Creed, that Jesus spent time in hell during the three days between his death and resurrection. The idea gets some mention in the New Testament, most notably in a couple of references in the book of Acts stating that Jesus wasn't "abandoned" to the grave,[14] and a statement, in 1 Peter, about Jesus preaching to

---

14. Acts 2:27, 31.

the spirits in prison.[15] The doctrine also draws from passages in the apocryphal Gospel of Nicodemus, which only pasty scholars and theologians read.

Traditionally, the "harrowing" part means Jesus invaded or despoiled the place by releasing the patriarchs—Abraham and Moses and other righteous folk who died before Jesus supplied the means of salvation to mankind—from an intermediate **Purgatory**-like state. Then Jesus triumphantly marched them right up to the Pearly Gates. Best upgrade ever.

Please use it in a sentence: If you ask a Christian to explain to you the "harrowing of hell," he or she will look at you funny, kind of like when you ask them to explain the line referring to it in the Apostle's Creed.

Not to be confused with: Any other jailbreaks, robberies, break-ins, or rescue attempts throughout history. Sorry, heist-movie wannabes. Your technological advancement and super-complicated timelines are impressive, but you just can't compete with the Son of God crashing the doors of hell in order to bust Elijah out of Satan's shackles.

❧ HINDUISM

The major faith tradition of India and the world's third largest religion behind Christianity and Islam, with nearly a billion practitioners. Its doctrines are spread across a pretty broad spectrum of theological beliefs, with schools of thought that might be described as **monotheistic**—there's one Absolute Reality behind everything, though it may show up in the form of different

---

15. 1 Peter 3:19–20, 4:6.

deities—and others that are flat-out **polytheistic.**[16] But most Hindus believe each person has a true self, the **atman,** which will be reincarnated from one body to another after death (**samsara**). The overall goal of the atman's existence is to attain **moksha,** or liberation, from the **karma**-related cycle. Yoga may or may not be involved.

More than 90 percent of the world's Hindus live in India and Nepal. An estimated one million Hindus live in the United States.

Hindus you've probably heard of: Deepak Chopra, Mahatma Gandhi, George Harrison, Aishwarya Rai, J. D. Salinger, M. Night Shyamalan, Vijay Singh.

🌿 INCORRUPT

Describing a body—usually that of a **saint**—that does not decompose, decay, stink, or otherwise perform as expected after death. A remarkable number of the corpses of Christian saints are believed to be incorrupt and are often on display at their shrines. To qualify, a body must remain inexplicably soft and flexible a substantial time after death. In order to figure out whether a body is incorrupt, of course, the remains must be exhumed. Which means that whole "rest in peace" thing? A total crock if you're holy.

Please use it in a sentence: The famously incorrupt body of Saint Catherine of Bologna, a Mother Superior who died in 1463, has been posed into a sitting position behind glass at her shrine at Bologna's Chapel of the Poor Clares, which isn't creepy at all.

Not to be confused with: The potentially nondecomposing, decay-resistant, surgically altered bodies of Hollywood residents. They're creepy, but they're not saints.

---

16. Some academics argue that Hinduism really shouldn't even be described as a religion. It's more like a crazy collection of related traditions, practices, and philosophies.

❧ ISLAM

Like **Christianity,** Islam is a monotheistic religion that evolved
from the life and teachings of an individual—in this case, the
prophet Muhammad, who was born in the sixth century and died
in the seventh, and who left behind a collection of revelatory writings known as the Qu'ran. Muslims pledge allegiance to God (Allah)
and Muhammad, and adhere to the **Five Pillars of Islam;** Muslims
hope to be resurrected after death and gain entrance to paradise,
called Jannah, based on their good works and the mercy of Allah.

Unfaithful Muslims will be doomed to Jahannam, the hell of
Islam, but will eventually be allowed into paradise based on Allah's
forgiveness. Non-Muslims have no such luck. For them, it's Jahannam forever.

Islam is the world's second largest religion, with an estimated
1.5 billion members divided among two main branches: the majority Sunni Muslims and minority Shi'a Muslims. It is the dominant
religion in North Africa and the Middle East.

Muslims you've probably heard of: Muhammad Ali, John
Coltrane, Mos Def, Osama bin Laden, Queen Noor, Malcolm X.

❧ JUDAISM

The monotheistic parent-religion of **Christianity,** dating back to
a shared lineage with the characters of Abraham, Isaac, and Jacob
described in the Torah (which Christians know as the first five
books of the Old Testament). Judaism claims an estimated 13 million people, spread across several divisions of practice and theology,
including Orthodox, Reform, Conservative, and Reconstructionist
versions. A primary distinction between Jews and Christians is that
Christians believe Jesus to be the long-awaited Messiah, come to

establish God's kingdom on earth. But Jews think Christians totally jumped to conclusions about Jesus and are still waiting for the Messiah to arrive.

Like most Christians and Muslims, Jews believe the soul is eternal and await **resurrection** in the world to come, the messianic age known as *Olam Haba*. The righteous hope to take up residence in *Gan Eden* (the "Garden of Eden"), but only the really holy people go there directly. Most require a brief stay in *Sheol,* or *Gehinnom,* where they are purified and/or punished for up to twelve months. But no longer than that. Which is good.

The majority of Jews live in the United States and Israel.

Jews you've probably heard of: Michael Bloomberg, Sascha Baron Cohen, Bob Dylan, Adam Sandler, Sarah Silverman, Stephen Spielberg.

🌿 KARMA

The law of cause and effect common to Indian religious traditions (Buddhism, Hinduism, Jainism, Sikhism), stating that the actions you take in this life have a bearing on the next one. All of your deeds—good, bad, and enormously stupid—have repercussions on your future lives and, in fact, the whole karmic enchilada is wrapped around your past and present lives as well. It's the circle of life, friends, and it doesn't end until you attain the liberated state of **moksha.**

The good news of karma is that, if you do good things, you'll be rewarded in your future **reincarnations.** You can expect an attractive spouse, a beautiful family, and above-average wealth and prestige. The bad news is that, if you do bad things, you'll be punished in a future life. You could end up a crippled beggar, or the guy who cleans the elephant cage at the zoo, or a reality-show contestant. So behave.

22

Please use it in a sentence: Achieving beneficial karma is like depositing cash (good deeds) into a savings account in order to go on a great vacation, except instead of going to Disneyworld once you've saved up enough, you just die and then wake up as a baby somewhere and have to endure several months of not being able to feed or otherwise care for yourself, and it's not long before you realize infancy is *so* not that fun and even good karma results in, like, the worst vacation ever.

Not to be confused with: *Kama Sutra,* the ancient Indian Sanskrit text on love, male–female relationships, and acrobatic sexual positions. Though it must be said that anyone who lives according to the *Kama Sutra* is most likely benefiting from some decent karma.

❧ MARTYR

A person who gets killed or executed for his or her faith, from the Greek word for "witness." In the early, persecution-heavy centuries of **Christianity,** martyrdom was frequent, and almost all of the Christian **saints** were martyrs. In **Islam,** adherents are expected to submit to the will of Allah, and part of this submission means a willingness to die if Allah has that in mind for them, especially while contending for the faith.

Whatever the religious system, martyrdom presupposes a belief in some kind of life after death—because why give up the material benefits of this life if there's not something to be gained on the other side? One of the benefits of Islamic martyrdom—particularly the controversial teachings that fuel violent extremists—is a guarantee of heaven.[17] And in

---

17. Based on Suras 4:74: "Whoso fighteth in the way of Allah, be he slain or be he victorious, on him We shall bestow a vast reward" (English translation by Mohammed Marmaduke Pickthall).

It's commonly reported that Islamic martyrs can expect to be blessed with seventy-two beautiful, virginal, sexual companions (houri) in the afterlife. This traditional number supposedly comes from a statement that someone once heard referenced by a companion of Muhammad, who apparently overheard the prophet mention something about the number of virgins—so it's a vague and grapeviney reference that's more of a myth than anything else. In fact, one expert compares this to the tradition that Christians will wear wings and play harps upon being granted entrance to heaven.[19]

heaven, of course, a good Muslim will be greeted by marriage to "fair ones with wide, lovely eyes."[18] And not just two or three of these fair ones, but a full harem of them. So that's something to look forward to.

Please use it in a sentence or two: During catechism, little Justine used to daydream about someday becoming a martyr, until she learned that it might involve having molten lead poured down your throat and iron hooks plunged into your intestines. So instead, she started daydreaming about ponies.

Not to be confused with: A suicide bomber.

❧ METEMPSYCHOSIS

A consonant-rich word from Greek philosophy referring to a concept called the "transmigration of souls," wherein a person's soul

---

18. Suras 44:54 (Pickthall). These "fair ones" are commonly known in Arabic as *houri*.
19. Nydell, Margaret K. *Understanding Arabs: A Guide for Modern Times* (Boston: Intercultural Press, Inc., 2006), p. 109.

shimmies from one body to another after physical death. This second body may be human, of course, but it also may be an animal or, lacking a better option, something inanimate. Like a houseplant. Or a scary vintage automobile. At any rate, *metempsychosis* is the word you use when **reincarnation** doesn't sound impressive enough, or when you want to name-drop Plato, who mentioned it in *The Republic.*

See also: *Reincarnation.*

❀ MOKSHA

The Sanksrit term referring to the emancipation of the **soul** from the cycle of living and dying and **reincarnation** and all those annoying aspects of earthly existence. Moksha is the state of release that all good Hindus, Buddhists, and other adherents of Indian religions strive for, except they may not precisely know it when they get there. Because experiencing the true nature of yourself and entering into a state of pure bliss in which you're no longer conscious of time and space but are instead enraptured by a profound oneness with the entire universe? It doesn't exactly happen within the limits of the five senses.

That's why moksha can only be achieved under the guidance of a guru who's achieved it himself. After all, someone has to tell you when to stop freeing yourself from the captivity of the material world so you can go grab a bite to eat.

Please use it in a sentence: Janet attends yoga in hopes of achieving moksha, but I'm mainly interested in achieving the ability to see my toes again.

Not to be confused with: *Mocha,* the drinking of which may involve a substantial amount of bliss. Even better, it's the kind that actually *does* operate within the five senses, because you can taste it, and smell it, and feel its luxurious warmth against the soft lines of your hand, and . . . oops, sorry. The *Pocket Guide* just about entered a state of oneness with the universe and had to pull back. This is just the first chapter, after all.

❧ MONOTHEISM

Belief in the existence of only one god, as opposed to **polytheism. Christianity, Islam,** and **Judaism** are examples of monotheistic religions.

    Please use it in a sentence: I'm down with monotheism, because it's hard enough to worship and obey one deity, let alone keep up with Krishna and Rama and Shiva and Kali and Ganesh and Ramachandra and all those other Hindu gods.

❧ MORMONISM

A new-ish, distinctively American religion founded by Joseph Smith Jr., when an angel named Moroni led him to the discovery of some golden tablets—written in "Reformed Egyptian"—buried back in the fifth century in Manchester, New York.[20] Smith's translation of those tablets led to the Book of Mormon, out of which arose the Church of Jesus Christ of Latter-Day Saints.

    Their beliefs have a few elements in common with **Christianity**— Mormons consider themselves followers of Jesus Christ—but they've tacked on a few creative enhancements. For instance, they think Jesus came to America after he resurrected (way before Columbus), which meant his earliest followers and the true Church developed among Native Americans. Other interesting Mormon

---

20. A place not generally known for its abundance of ancient "Reformed Egyptian" artifacts. See pp. 68–69 in Chapter 3 for more about Joseph Smith.

beliefs include eternal marriage, baptisms for dead people, the eventual transformation of believers into gods, strict abstinence from alcohol and caffeine, and the necessity of polygamy—which used to be a big part of the faith but is no longer tolerated, except among crazy fundamentalist Mormons and on HBO.

There are nearly 13 million Mormons worldwide. Approximately half of them live in the United States.

Mormons you've probably heard of: Wilford Brimley, Orson Scott Card, Butch Cassidy, Steven R. Covey, Jon Heder, Katherine Heigl, Donnie and Marie Osmond, Mitt Romney, Ricky Schroder.

⚜ MUMMIFICATION

See *Embalming*.

⚜ NEAR-DEATH EXPERIENCE

A series of sensations related to imminent death, often involving levitation, bright lights, the singing of angels, warmth and security, some sort of life review involving the phrase "flashed before my eyes," reunions with dead relatives, encounters with Jesus, and even the feeling of being separate from one's body. And mixed into the experience of any of these elements is a sense that you're already dead.

Near-death experiences have been documented by people undergoing surgery, being resuscitated from heart attacks, or suffering life-threatening accidents. Such experiences are either (1) totally legitimate albeit paranormal windows into the afterlife or (2) nothing more than brain-generated hallucinations. It depends upon who's telling the story. Option 1 is lots more fun, and the *Pocket Guide* has a fondness for bright, warm floatingness, so for now, it's the winner.

Please use it in a sentence: Jared has an irrational fear of having a near-death experience, so one way to really freak him out is to shine a flashlight in his face and start yelling "The light! The light!"

Not to be confused with: *Near-Birth Experience,* an actual phenomenon in which people claim to remember events occurring before conception, or during the process of birth, or while in the womb. You might know this by its other name: *making up crap.*

☙ NECROMANCY

The ancient and spooky practice of trying to summon the deceased (or, in some cases, demons) in order to receive knowledge about the future, based on the idea that supernatural beings have secret access to information, on account of them not being bound to the normal physical constraints of space and time. Necromancy isn't practiced much anymore—it's too complicated, what with all those complex incantations and cryptic symbols and ritual sacrifices that pretty much only appeal to upper-level Wiccans—but it was a big deal back in the Middle Ages.

Please use it in a sentence: When I saw Lucy and her friends attempting to call forth the spirit of Don Knotts from inside a circle made of strips of squirrel flesh, I said to myself, "Necromancy!" and put a stop to that devilry.

Not to be confused with: *Nephomancy,* the interpretive art of divination using clouds to recognize omens or foretell the future. Nephomancy is perhaps most accurate when the future has soft, white, and/or fluffy qualities.

☙ NEGATIVE CONFESSION

A recited moral code appearing in the Egyptian *Book of the Dead.* The confessor lists a variety of misdeeds he has *not* performed—thus the "negative"—in order to be allowed entrance to the afterlife. The list is forty-two confessions long, including gems like *I have not slain men and women, I have made none to weep, I have not stolen cultivated land, I have not eaten the heart, I have not been an eavesdropper,* and *I have never raised my voice.*

Sure, you haven't slain anyone, but have you *eavesdropped*? Hard-core, those Egyptians.

After the confession, the person's heart was removed, placed on a scale, and weighed in relation to a feather. If it weighed more than a feather, it was still too full of sin. Entrance to paradise? Denied. And that's "denied" in the sense of getting eaten by the ferocious demon Ammut.[21]

Not to be confused with: *The Ten Commandments,* another listy moral code that came around a few centuries later and which some academics suggest may have been influenced—along with all its *thou shalt nots*—by the Negative Confession.[22]

🌿 NIRVANA

The definition of *nirvana* depends largely on the perspective of the person trying to achieve it. A Hindu seeking nirvana is looking to snuff out his full spectrum of attachment to the physical world—escaping passion, ignorance, anger, and hip-hop ringtones—so that his **soul,** or **atman,** can experience union with the divine. Nirvana is the empty, peaceful road toward the destination known as **moksha.**

A Buddhist believes the part about the soul is just a lot of silly talk, because the soul doesn't really exist anyway. And guess what?

---

21. See p. 104 for details.
22. These same academics tend to cower when they make this suggestion, because who wants to go on record calling God a plagiarist?

For him, *nirvana* can be defined as finally beginning to understand, for yourself, the whole thing about the soul not existing.

So now you know: there is no soul. Next step? Pull out your lifetime to-do list. Find the one that says: *Achieve a state of transcendental rest and liberation from temporal awareness.* And scratch that baby off.

You're welcome.

Please use it in a sentence: I was all excited about experiencing Nirvana once in the early '90s, but it turned out to be some lame cover band.

No, really, quit joking: We could tell the yogi was experiencing nirvana because he didn't even flinch when Craig shanked his Frisbee throw and the disc bounced right off the dude's forehead.

⚜ POLYTHEISM

Belief in the existence of multiple gods, as opposed to **monotheism. Hinduism** is often described as a polytheistic religion, with many gods either in service to the supreme deity, Brahman, or existing as various incarnations of Brahman.

Some suggest **Buddhism** is also polytheistic, since its texts speak

It's been stated before that there are 330 million gods in Hinduism, which is about 330 million too many to keep up with. That's not really the case, though. The Bhagavad Gita, a Hindu scripture, teaches that God dwells in the atman of each human. And at one point it was believed that there were 330 million people in the world, thus 330 million "gods" hanging out in all those atmans. It's sort of like saying there are 2 billion Jesuses because the Savior dwells in the heart of every Christian on earth.

of powerful supernatural beings like *deva*s and *bodhisattva*s and since it tends to incorporate a full salad bar of local deities into its belief system. But others argue that Buddhism is an atheistic religion—one that denies any kind of eternal supreme being altogether. It's quite the controversy. But at least it's a transcendentally peaceful one.

Please use it in a sentence: Buddhism may be confusing, but Greek mythology provides a clear example of polytheism, thanks to Zeus, Apollo, Aphrodite, and that whole dysfunctional bunch of Olympians.

PREDESTINATION

The idea that a person's actions and eternal destiny have been divinely foreordained from the moment of creation, based on a belief in God's omniscience and control over the universe. One person will be saved and given a pre-punched ticket for heaven. Another finds out he's already booked on the smoky train. And there's nothing either passenger can do about it.

In Christianity, the hardest-of-hard-core beliefs in predestination are usually associated with the teachings of the sixteenth-century reformer John Calvin. In Islam, it's standard teaching that nothing happens outside the will of Allah, who ordains everything—including one's eternal destiny.

Please use it in a sentence: You might hear a believer in predestination say things like "If Allah wills . . ." or "God has a plan for me" or "Why even bother?"

Not to be confused with: *Prestidigitation*—otherwise known as sleight-of-hand—which can be, in the expert hands of some practitioners, on the spine-chilling verge of seeming supernatural.

But it won't earn you a place in heaven, no matter how good you are at the Zarrow Shuffle.[23]

🌿 PURGATORY

A teaching of Roman Catholic **Christianity** that there is a middle ground between heaven and hell for those who died as believers but still had a few lingering—yet totally forgivable—sins to eliminate. In short, Purgatory acts as a post-death purification to clean you up for heaven. Sounds good, but Protestant Christians think this is a lot of bunk. First, they argue, it's not really in the Bible. And second, aren't you clean enough anyway, thanks to the forgiveness of Jesus?

Please use it in a sentence or two: You might argue that the temporary, purifying flames of Purgatory are way preferable to the eternal, punishing flames of hell, but I'm pretty sure flames of any persuasion are not much fun.

Not to be confused with: *Predatory,* a word used to describe anything related to a predator. It is likely that no one would ever confuse this with Purgatory, unless the rules changed, and instead of a person's sins being purified by fire, they were instead devoured by large jungle cats. Which would be awesome to contemplate but still not too enjoyable.

Also not to be confused with: *Limbo,* which is another theoretical middle ground in Christian theology, and which is described in greater detail on p. 112 in chapter 4.

🌿 REINCARNATION

The belief that some independent, essential, nonphysical part of personhood—for instance, the **soul,** or the self—survives physical

---

23. Shout-out: card trick nerds!

death only to find its way into another body and another lifetime. Known by the Sanskrit term *samsara,* the cycle of rebirth from one life into the next is central to Eastern religions like **Hinduism**, Jainism, and Taoism. You might think that reincarnation was also central to **Buddhism,** but you'd be wrong on a technicality, because Buddhists don't believe in a permanent soul. Replace soul with "consciousness," though, and Buddhists are totally on-board.

Anyway, reincarnation is probably most prevalent in Hinduism. Within this system, the cycle of birth and death and soul-transfer continues until a being finally realizes that his or her true self isn't really about the outward body, or its pleasures, or its demands, but instead has to do with the inward, immortal soul. This is called **moksha.** And once you get there, all the rein-

Some West African traditions believe families may be plagued by "repeater children"—souls that keep being reborn into the same family following the deaths of infants. Wow. Just composing that sentence gave the Pocket Guide *chills.*

carnating stops and you can rest. Hopefully by this point, your **karma** has earned you the body of a supermodel, as opposed to, say, a dung beetle. Because it's easier to rest when you're spectacularly hot.

Please use it in a sentence: Jeff figured his cat-like reflexes, passion for tuna, and general aversion to authority were evidence of his previous reincarnation from an Egyptian housecat into the body of an accountant.

Not to be confused with: *Carnation Instant Breakfast,* a creamy, delicious health drink containing essential vitamins and minerals.

Unfortunately, there's nothing "creamy" or "delicious" about reincarnation. Unless you come back as pudding.

❧ RESURRECTION

The ultimate goal of **Christianity, Judaism,** and **Islam,** in which eternal **souls** will eventually be restored to some form of their original, individual selves in order to enjoy eternity. Christians base this belief on the resurrection of Jesus Christ three days after his crucifixion, including the expectation that Christ's Second Coming includes physical resurrection of dead believers—and that those new bodies will get to participate in the "new heaven and new earth," as described in the New Testament book of Revelation.[24]

Judaism also carries the hope of resurrection when the Messiah—not Jesus, thank you very much—finally appears, ushering them into his eternal kingdom. Islam teaches a universal resurrection at the world's end, followed by the division at Judgment between faithful Muslims and infidels, with everyone going their separate ways in their resurrected bodies. And Zoroastrians get into resurrection a little, too, but how many Zoroastrians do you really know?

Please use it in a sentence or two: Fearful he'd be left with nothing to reanimate at the resurrection, Belinda took a hard stand against Uncle Charlie's cremation. She also took a hard stand against him leaving all his money to the Baptist church, but that was less successful.

Not to be confused with: *Zombies.*

---

24. Revelation 21:1.

🌿 SAINT

In **Christianity,** a term used to describe any follower of Jesus, from the Latin word *sanctus,* which means holy or consecrated. But the most popular use of *saint* refers to a righteous person recognized in an official capacity by the Church for having displayed impressive holiness and virtue. Most saints are viewed as being just as active post-death as they were before meeting their Maker. Saints perform miracles; watch over the cities, churches, occupations, and illnesses over which they've been made patrons; and assist living humans in getting prayers delivered to (and answered by) God. It's assumed that they're experts at this kind of thing because they're (1) super-holy, (2) already dead, and (3) probably tighter with the Almighty than you.

Please use it in a sentence or two: Confronted with a nasty pimple outbreak the day before the prom, Eliza appealed to Saint Anthony the Abbot, patron saint of skin diseases, to clear up her complexion. And with Anthony's assistance—not to mention a thick application of concealer—everything turned out just fine.

Not to be confused with: *Gus Van Sant,* who may not be on speaking terms with God, but might be able to pull some strings, in a pinch, with Kevin Smith.

🌿 SALVATION

The ultimate and eternal goal of the practitioners of most world religions, despite there being (apparently) a bunch of different ways to achieve it. Christians view salvation as the free gift of deliverance from **sin,** made possible through faith in Jesus Christ, based on his death and **resurrection.** Jews anticipate salvation in their longing for a coming Messiah. Muslims rely on their adherence to the **Five Pillars of Islam** and the mercy of Allah on the day of judgment.

Buddhists and Hindus don't really view salvation through the lens of sin and judgment, but rather as something that may be achieved through enlightenment, **nirvana, moksha,** or other words you might hear in yoga class.

Please use it in a sentence or two: In his pursuit of salvation, Chuck has become, in order, a practicing Jew, Christian, Muslim, Hindu, and Buddhist. What he forgot to become was a decent guy.

Not to be confused with: *Salivation.* That extra "i" is pretty important when it comes to your eternal destiny.[25]

⚜ SAMSARA

See *Reincarnation.*

⚜ SÉANCE

A meeting of spiritual-minded folks for the purpose of communicating with the dead. Usually, a medium is present to smooth the communication process, as ghosts and regular living people don't always speak on the same wavelength. This medium—usually a person with (alleged) psychic gifts, who may or may not be a professional[26]—may go into a trance or write unconsciously on a pad or perform an interpretive dance in order to relay some message from the beyond.

Séances became popular in the late 1800s and early 1900s, thanks to an explosion of interest in spirit communication beginning with the media attention surrounding the Fox Sisters (see p. 69 in Chapter 3) and other notable spiritualists.

---

25. Except for Buddhists, who don't believe in the existence of the "I." Rimshot!
26. . . . and who may or may not be a total fraud (if history is any indicator).

Please use it in a sentence or two: It's best to turn the lights down during a séance, or to rely only on candlelight, because ghosts are more comfortable in dark rooms. Also, low light makes it lots easier for fraudulent mediums to fake the spooky stuff.

Not to be confused with: *Beyoncé,* who also does her best work in dark rooms but who rarely imparts information from the beyond. Unless one considers bootyliciousness an example of otherworldly communication.

🌿 SIN

In Christian, Jewish, and Islamic theology, any thought, word, or action that is contrary to God's plan or commandments. Traditionally, Christians view sin as *universal* (everyone does it) and *pervasive* (it can pop up anywhere at any time during any activity, even while—*crap,* there it goes). Even further, sin is not just a choice—a refusal to live according to God's desires—but a condition of humanity. We're born into it, and it's a barrier between people and God.[27] This understanding of sin is rejected by Judaism and Islam, however, which view it as more of an individual action than a universal condition.

In terms of the afterlife, people who die in a sinful state are thought to be headed for hell, where they'll be punished. Christian believers who trust Jesus Christ for the forgiveness of their sins go to heaven. Faithful Muslims go to heaven, too. But probably not the same heaven as Christians, because that would be awkward.

Please use it in a sentence or two: Is it a sin to lust after candy bars? Because I would totally risk eternal damnation for a mouthful of chewy nougat.

---

27. This is known in Christianity as the doctrine of original sin, based on scriptural passages like Romans 5:12.

Not to be confused with: *Sin,* the ancient bearded Babylonian moon god who rode around on a flying bull. He's neither universal, pervasive, or . . . real.

❧ SIN EATERS

In ye olden days in the British Isles, people who died with unforgiven sin were thought to wander around in a type of Purgatory, unable to enjoy paradise or bliss until they had been freed from their sins. So a person called the "sin eater" would perform the ritual of consuming a small amount of bread and drink at a person's death bed, a symbolic action that transferred the dying person's sin upon himself. This weirdly metaphorical practice lasted until the early 1900s.

Please use it in a sentence: Caught sneaking a hot dog into a memorial service for his great aunt Lydia, Michael tried to excuse his behavior by telling everyone he was a sin eater.

Not to be confused with: *Eating* for recreational or nutritional purposes.[28]

❧ SOUL

The internal essence of a living being that, in many religious and/ or philosophical systems, is immortal and survives in some form after death—where it may be judged, rewarded, punished, ferried across a metaphorical underground river, or launched into another physical body via **reincarnation.** Modern science is skeptical about the existence of an immortal soul, preferring to refer to it as "consciousness" or "the mind" or "the thing Voldemort divided up into horcruxes."

---

28. Admit it: You totally thought the *Pocket Guide* would go with "Death Eaters" here, from the Harry Potter books. Nerd.

Please use it in a sentence or two: When Dan told us he'd sold his soul to the Devil in exchange for immortality, we laughed because Dan was such a joker, until Dan's eyes turned yellow, his head spun around, and he incinerated Lester with a blast of sulfuric breath. We didn't laugh then, because the joke had gone way too far.

Not to be confused with: *Soul,* the musical love-child of the funky relationship between gospel music and rhythm and blues, and of whom James Brown is the godfather.

In the early 1900s, citing the results of a series of highly disputed scientific experiments that were actually reported in the New York Times, a Massachusetts physician named Duncan MacDougall announced that a person lost approximately 21 grams in mass at the moment of death. That amount represented the weight of the soul, he hypothesized, and the difference was due to the soul exiting the body. It makes for a cool anecdote, if you leave out the part where a crazy Scottish doctor won't let you die in peace but keeps hoisting you up onto a scale every time you let out a death-wheeze.

THANATOLOGY

The academic study of dying and death as it relates to humans, from *Thanatos,* the Greek god of death.[29] As far as scientific disciplines go, it's a fairly new one that hardly existed until the turn of the twentieth century. Even then, it didn't catch on much until World War II, when suddenly death was on everyone's mind.

---

29. He had a twin brother named Hypnos, the god of sleep. "Oh, great," the other deities used to say. "Here come Thanatos and Hypnos. Those guys are such downers."

Thanatology engages a variety of disciplines, from sociology and psychology to medicine and theology. Despite this breadth, it maintains a pretty low profile. After all, very few people like to think about death, so no one's exactly dying to get into the field. (Sorry.)

Please use it in a sentence or two: When Don told us he was pursuing a career in thanatology, we responded the way anyone would. We told him to quit making up fields of study.

Not to be confused with: _Thanos,_ the fictional alien supervillain from the Marvel Comics universe. He's well acquainted with death, too, but not in a professional or metaphorical way. It's more of a literal "let me introduce you to my lovely female companion, Death" kind of way.

❧ ZOMBIE

A soulless reanimated corpse, typically made that way thanks to a supernatural spell, a science experiment gone wrong, a killer disease, or George Romero. Zombies either move really slowly or blindingly fast, sport tattered clothing and decomposing flesh, and can't communicate further than a baleful grunt or harrowing moan.

You probably think zombies only exist in movies, but adherents of the Voodoo folk religion believe the dead can be revived by powerful wicked sorcerers.[30] So try not to die around any powerful wicked Voodoo sorcerers.

Please use it in a sentence or two: Don't bother speaking to Lesley before her first cup of coffee. She's a total zombie, and not the freakish, high-speed kind, either.

Not to be confused with: _Rob Zombie,_ the heavy-metal musician, film director, and all-around horror enthusiast. Try not to die around him, either.

---

30. See p. 61 in Chapter 3 for more Voodoo/zombie fun.

CHAPTER 2

Great Moments in Eternity, Part 1

(A Timeline: 2000 B.C.E. to 1563)

Over the last few millennia, there have been plenty of things about which humans have disagreed. Like whether Ginger or Mary Ann was hotter. Or whether or not the New York Yankees are, in fact, evil. Or whether or not heaven is located in the sky, in another dimension, in the presence of God Almighty, or in the branches of a big honking tree.[1] But there is one thing agreed upon by cultures ancient and modern, primitive and sophisticated, large and small: it's that mankind will encounter some sort of existence beyond the one we're experiencing right now.

Some of these ideas—resurrection of the body, blissful paradise, peaceful sleep—sound pretty nice. Other ideas are less appealing, unless you get your ya-yas from the possibility of eternal, conscious,

---

1. See the 250 C.E. entry on p. 54.

fiery torment. Either way, people have spent a lot of time fearing death, and thinking about death, and cultivating intricate traditions about what happens on the other side of death.

Here, then, are some of the most notable moments in our lengthy obsession with the Great Unknown. You'll not be surprised to discover the history of the afterlife is as varied as the human race. And pretty much just as weird.

2000 B.C.E., MESOPOTAMIA

An ancient poet writes an ancient poem now known as the Epic of Gilgamesh. It's one of humanity's most famous works of literature and the oldest recorded hero tale. It's also a crackling story, because Gilgamesh is history's first action hero. He's a superhuman king who slays the Bull of Heaven. He's a half-divine ruler who rejects the advances of the goddess Ishtar. Also, he's complicated. Because between the scenes of romance and adventure, Gilgamesh spends a lot of time pondering his own mortality. He's knee-deep in his own Mesopotamian culture, of course, so he views the afterlife as pretty much what you'd expect from a primitive culture dedicated to ground burial. Death, he believes, involves a lot of dust, a lot of darkness, and a lot of general horribleness. It pretty much sucks compared to an earthly life in which love goddesses throw themselves at you and you kill a sacred bull and poets write epic poems about you.

Having preoccupied himself with death, Gil does all he can to avoid it. He attempts to gain eternal life from a Noah-like hero named Utnapishtim (some call him "Tim"), who survived a great flood and thus defeated death. Utnapishtim tests Gilgamesh to see if he's worthy of immortality. A serpent is involved. Gilgamesh fails, and discovers he's less superhuman than he thought. But in the end, our hero ends up learning a timely lesson: People die, and it makes us sad, but that's how the world works. He decides to enjoy the life he's got, which is a good suggestion for everyone. He also determines not to focus too much on death. Which is also a good suggestion, but one the *Pocket Guide* prefers you ignore until you've finished this book.

1600 B.C.E., EGYPT

Pyramids! Tombs! Sarcophagi! The people of ancient Egypt begin to perfect their elaborate burial techniques and customs, all for the purpose of guaranteeing a soul's survival beyond death. And what sorts of procedures help the soul survive death? Well, mummification, for one. And the removal of the brain and other internal organs. And stuffing the leftover organ cavities like a Thanksgiving turkey, only a whole lot nastier, and with spice-laden wads of cloth instead of seasoned bread crumbs. Another practice is the inclusion of valuables, food, and other items in the tomb. Because in the afterlife, you never know when you might need, for instance, eight baskets of fruit.[2]

It's around this time that the first "Books of the Dead" begin to show up. They're placed within arm's reach of the deceased to help them pass through the underworld and into the paradise of Aaru, the Field of Reeds. You probably already read about the Egyptian *Book of the Dead*—known more accurately, but far less intimidatingly, as *Going Forth by Day*—on p. 7 in the first chapter.[3]

---

2. The fruit baskets are among the items found in the famous tomb of King Tutankhamun.

3. Unless you were skipping around or something. Which is totally fine, as long as you don't get confused.

1500 B.C.E., EGYPT[4]

Keeping with the death-in-ancient-Egypt theme, the Angel of
Death arrives at the Nile Delta to perform the dramatic final act of
the ten plagues, as told in the Old Testament book of Exodus. The
angel passes over Egypt, killing all the first-born sons of the Egyptians but sparing those Israelite families who have smeared the blood
of a lamb upon their doorposts. This leads to the Jews' Moses-guided
mass exodus out of Egypt. It also leads to the traditional Jewish Pass-
over celebration. And the idea of a death-dealing angel *also* leads to
the development of the Western idea of the Grim Reaper, which is
the concept behind the hit 1976 hit song "(Don't Fear) the Reaper"
by Blue Oyster Cult, which provides the musical setting for the
famous *Saturday Night Live* skit in 2000 that introduces the catch-
phrase "more cowbell!" to popular culture, and which therefore
confirms the ancient Mayan prophecies predicting a direct, mystical
link between Moses and Will Ferrell.[5]

1000 B.C.E., INDIA

The earliest elements of Hinduism begin to emerge from the
historical Vedic religion, a loose set of beliefs stemming from the ancient religious texts (called *Vedas*) of India. These texts—the *Rigveda,
Yarjuveda, Samaveda,* and *Artharvaveda*—are primarily filled with
ritual instructions, chants, prayers, hymns, and liturgical verses. What

---

4. Because it's based on dating derived from the Scriptures, this date is disputed.
Especially by people who think the idea of an Angel of Death is a little fanciful to
begin with.

5. Not a real prophecy.

you won't find in these texts is a whole lot of traditional teaching about reincarnation, at least not in the way most contemporary Hindus understand it.

The earliest Hindu religion was pretty vague about it. There's a little talk about a dead soul making an afterlife passage to the "World of the Fathers" in the sky, where he or she then receives a new heavenly body. The souls were bodiless, of course, because they had been cremated at death. Then, as the centuries pass, people place more and more emphasis on this new body thing. Survivors of the deceased begin to believe their specific actions in the physical world help create and maintain that new afterlife body. A bunch of special post-cremation rituals develop because folks want to make sure their heavenly chassis isn't a lemon. *Don't light the wrong candles, son, or Grandpa will end up with an octopus tentacle for an arm.* The good old karmic death-and-rebirth cycle grows out of these early Vedic traditions.

800 B.C.E., GREECE

Homer writes the *Odyssey,* the epic ancient Greek poem following Odysseus as he tries to get home to Ithaca after the Trojan War. Along with Homer's *Iliad* (the story of the war itself) the *Odyssey* is one of the foundational texts of Western literature. Odysseus goes to a lot of places on this journey and sees lots of things—a Cyclops, beautiful Sirens, a bunch of pig-sailors—but central to the *Pocket Guide*'s purposes is the scene where he's sent to the Land of the Dead on an info-gathering assignment. He finds it at the far west end of the ocean. When he gets there, Odysseus sacrifices some sheep; pours out offerings of honey, milk, water, and wine; engages in conversation with a bunch of random spirits; and receives instructions from dead friends and family. Certain members of the welcoming party give him advice about returning home, but only after they've drunk the blood of the sacrificed sheep. Because this unlocks their ability to speak to Odysseus.

Keep this in mind the next time you attend a funeral. Sure, Uncle Chester looks all creepy and overly made-up in the open casket, but at least no one's slicing open a sheep and handing you a bloody shot glass prior to the viewing.

POSSIBLY 600 B.C.E., PERSIA

The last shall be first. Long consigned to the alphabetical tail of the world religions list, Zoroastrianism is actually one of history's first recorded religions. Most traditions date it around the sixth century B.C.E., though some historians place it as early as several thousand years before Christ. So the *Pocket Guide* is not entirely certain where to list it on the timeline, but we're sure of a couple things. First, the Zorofaith is founded by the world's most famous Z-named religious figure, Zoroaster (also known as Zarathustra),[6] who starts out as a nomadic tribesman in ancient Persia before firing up a side gig as a religious prophet. Second, the movement that develops around his teachings ends up becoming one of the first religions to speculate on the immortality of the soul.

Zoroaster believes in a variety of deities, but the main one, Ahura Mazda, promises to resurrect the righteous and give them immortal,

---

6. Zarathustra is the real name. Zoroaster is only the name the ancient Greeks gave him. Still, Zoroaster is preferred. For one thing, the religious tradition named after him is called Zoroastrianism. Which is hard enough to say anyway. "Zarathustrianism" is well-nigh impossible. For the record, Nietzsche was a fan of the original name, titling one of his most famous books *Thus Spake Zarathustra*.

youthful bodies. Then they get to live forever in peace and harmony in a perfect paradise. The unrighteous get consumed by fire at the Judgment after having been tortured for ages in a hellish realm. Sound familiar? That's because many scholars think his dualistic, good-versus-evil, resurrection-and-final-judgment worldview has a direct influence on religions with ties to the same area. Like Islam. And Judaism. And Christianity. (Keep reading.) There are still a few thousand Zoroastrians in Iran and India today. They're now known as Parsis. It's easier to say.

600 B.C.E., INDIA

A prince named Siddhartha Guatama Buddha—also known by other random combinations of those three names—founds Buddhism, an offshoot of early Hinduism. Siddy G is mostly in tune with the traditional Hindu ideas about reincarnation and karma, except for one specific doctrine that sticks in his fat-bellied craw: he doesn't believe humans have eternal souls. Sure, we *think* we do. But we're wrong. What we really have, he teaches, is a collection of desires and sensations and memories that seem *kinda* soul-ish because they cluster together as we pass from body to body. But all that stuff is just a big delusion. Once we abandon this delusion, we break free of the false self and are liberated from the process of reincarnation. Yay!

According to tradition, the Buddha's final words before dying were "All composite things pass away. Strive for your own liberation with diligence."

After that, we just dissolve into nothingness. Oh. Thanks for the enlightenment, Buddha.

49

360 B.C.E., GREECE

In Plato's most famous work, *Republic,* the great Greek philosopher holds forth on an embarrassing variety of things you don't know nearly enough about, like the best qualities of certain forms of government. And the worst things about other types of government. And the nature of knowledge and justice. And how ultimate reality might be described allegorically as the difference between seeing shadows flickering on the wall of a cave and actually seeing real stuff in the light of the world outside the cave. It's seriously profound. But none of that stuff's important when compared to . . . Platonic life-after-death stories!

In Book X, Plato tells of a slain Pamphylian soldier named Er. Unfortunately, Er gets killed in battle. He's been dead for, like, two weeks. Then Er wakes up—exceedingly *not* dead—right there at the top of his funeral pyre. This is awkward at first. But then Er starts telling everyone about his fascinating near-death experience. It seems his soul, along with a bunch of other souls, mystically road-tripped to a place where they encountered these big openings in the ground and sky. Divine judges sat next to these openings like celestial traffic cops, telling people where to go. Er watched the righteous head upward and rightward to a place of beauty and delight. The bad tumbled down and left to a realm of suffering where they were punished tenfold for each of their sins. But eventually, both the righteous and unrighteous passed out of these worlds and into a new one, in which they are reincarnated as humans or animals. Once Er figures this out, he's dispatched back to the land of the living so he can spread the word about what he's seen. First priority? Tell Plato. Dude's got influence.

STILL 360-ISH B.C.E., GREECE

Plato writes another masterpiece, his *Apology,* which follows the arguments and thoughts of his mentor, Socrates, as he defends himself in a trial. A serious trial—he's accused of corrupting the young and being an atheist. Upon being declared guilty, Socrates is forced to execute himself by drinking hemlock. But Socrates refuses to go gently into that good night, not when there are speeches to give and conundrums to explore. So, hemlock in hand, he holds forth on the nature of death. He proposes that death must truly be one of life's great blessings. Because it's either a whole eternity of dreamless nothingness—which sounds kinda peaceful compared to the Roman rat race—or it's an otherworldly dimension where you can shoot the philosophical bull with the great figures of history, like Homer. Or Odysseus. Sounds heavenly . . . at least for Socrates. Perhaps not for Homer, though. Because that Socrates could be a real blowhard.

According to Plato, Socrates' last words before dying were, "Crito, we owe a cock to Asclepius. Pay it and do not neglect it." Socrates totally missed Buddha's memo about profundity at the moment of death.

BETWEEN 200 B.C.E. AND 200 C.E., INDIA

The *Bhagavad Gita* is composed and inserted into an overly long poem called the *Mahabharata,*[7] making it even longer. But it's a worthwhile addition, because the B-G becomes one of the most

---

7. The *Mahabharata* is one of the longest epic poems in history and a central Hindu scripture.

influential texts of Hinduism. Nutshell: it's a seven-hundred-verse conversation between the warrior Arjuna and his chariot driver, the god Krishna. It's the night before a great battle, but Arjuna's having second thoughts. His conscience gets the best of him—what with all the killing and stuff that takes place in battles—so he refuses to fight. Krishna will have none of this. He explains to Arjuna that the soul and the body aren't the same thing. In fact, the soul reincarnates, so it never really dies. Which means you might destroy a few bodies now and then, but you can never really kill anyone. As in *kill* kill. So there's no need, silly warrior Arjuna, to be concerned about the ethics of death and dismemberment and all that combat frivolity. Just pick up your sword and swing away. Leave the guilt behind.

Obviously, this is where Mahatma Ghandi, the famous Hindu leader, got all his radical ideas about nonviolence.

165 B.C.E., BABYLON

The first in a long line of apocalyptic literature, the Old Testament book of Daniel is written and/or assembled. Part of Daniel dates from the Babylonian Exile around the sixth century B.C.E. Other elements suggest it should be dated in the second century B.C.E., during a period of persecution in which the Jews are subject to the Syro-Greek rule of the Seleucids.[8] Regardless of the time frame, historians believe the Jewish people no doubt come into contact with Zoroastrianism, which happens to be the primary religion of their Babylonian captors. Or Seleucid oppressors. Anyway, it seems a few of old Zoroaster's good-versus-evil teachings may have rubbed

---

8. You might have heard this referred to as the Antiochian persecution, but only if you spend excessive time with history nerds.

off on Israel, because the book of Daniel is full of dreams and revelations and freaky descriptions of his vision of the last days. And smack in the middle of those details is a shiny new concept that, up to this point, has been absent from the Jewish tradition. The big idea? Resurrection.[9]

No longer do the Hebrew people fear some nebulous existence in *Sheol,* a dark post-death dreamworld. Nope. Now they look forward to a sparkly, happy extension of this *actual* world, in the same old (but somehow renewed) physical bodies they used to have. But this new doctrine, while exciting enough, raises several deep questions:

Is resurrection a legitimate afterlife?
Or is it more like a continuation of present life?
And what happens if you get cremated?

Burning questions, indeed.

40 C.E., JERUSALEM

The probable date for the crucifixion and resurrection of Jesus Christ, the proclaimed tipping point that explodes Christianity from an obscure Jewish sect into a dominant Western religion. Among Christians, the idea of resurrection presupposes a belief that the soul is immortal and will someday, somewhere, somehow reunite with the resurrected body.

---

9. See Daniel 12:2: "Multitudes who sleep in the dust of the earth will awake: some to everlasting life, others to shame and everlasting contempt."

90 C.E., PATMOS

The Apostle John, in exile on the isle of Patmos, has a vision of the end of the world. He writes it down. This is fortuitous, as his dreamy letter ends up putting the showstopping touches—scriptural jazz hands, if you will—on the New Testament. How? By describing deathly plagues, apocalyptic battles, fiery acts of destruction, and highly memorable descriptions of hell ("They will be tormented day and night for ever and ever") and heaven ("There will be no more death or mourning or crying or pain . . .").[10] John also depicts heaven as a perfect 1,400-mile-wide cube made of gold. But people tend to forget that detail.

If a 1,400-mile-wide cube were plopped down in the middle of the united states, it would stretch from Mexico to canada and from the california border all the way into a good section of the Appalachian mountains. But it would be sorta wobbly due to the Rockies.

250 C.E., YUCATAN PENINSULA

The ancient Mayan civilization hits its glory years, as the oldest of the big three ancient high cultures of the Americas (along with the Incans and Aztecs). The Mayans have a whole lot of developed ideas about math and astronomy and the calendar, as these things are interesting to people who see life as being cyclical. The Mayans also have a whole lot of developed ideas about the value of human

---

10. Revelation 20:10 and 21:4, respectively.

sacrifice, which is also interesting but in a way that makes people feel a little squeamish.

Not quite as developed, though, are any Mayan notions about what actually happens once the sacrificial victim dies, seconds after his still-beating heart has been viciously cut out of his chest and plucked from his body as a sacrifice to the gods. What we do know about the Mayan afterlife is that they believe certain people gain immortality after death. These include priests, warriors who die on the battlefield, women who die during childbirth, and those who kill themselves by hanging. Really. If your death puts you in one of these categories, you get to dwell in paradise, located within the heavenly branches of the cosmic tree of life (whose roots, of course, reach down into the underworld). But if you're just a lowly victim of sacrifice? Or if you kill yourself in a nonsanctioned manner? Bad news in this life *and* the next.

600-ISH c.e., ENGLAND

If you're into pagan burial grounds—and honestly, who's not?— you'll love this. Sometime around the sixth century, the first of twenty "princely" burials is thought to have taken place at Sutton Hoo, a unique mega-graveyard along a Suffolk river bank near East Anglia, England. Despite having been subject to multiple plunderings over the centuries, the site gets rediscovered in 1938 by its landowner, thanks to the suggestion of her totally nonfraudulent dowsing nephew.[11] *You know all those mounds on your land, auntie?*

---

11. Dowsing: the mystical skill of "divining" the existence of water or precious metals underground, using (in most cases) that noted scientific apparatus, the Y-shaped stick. Dowsing is usually thought to be a lot of quackery. Usually.

My magical dowsing rod informs me there is something beneath them.
Turns out he's right, and then some. One of the mounds is found to
contain a ninety-foot-long boat in a trenched-out wooden chamber.
The boat is filled with gold, other precious metals, and the remains
of a dead warrior complete with war-making accessories. These
include his sword, shield, scepter, clothing, and a pot of gold. The
mystery dead guy is thought to have been the East Anglian king
Raedwald, who died around 625. Other mounds reveal children
buried with spears and men cremated with deer and horses. Nice
job, nephew-with-a-stick.

610 c.e., A CAVE OUTSIDE MECCA

An orphan and merchant in Mecca named Abu l-Qasim Muhammad ibn 'Abd Allah al-Hashimi al-Qurashi—you probably know
him by his shorter street name, *Muhammad*—becomes disillusioned
with the hubbub of Mecca and isolates himself in a desert cave at
the age of twenty-six. He starts meditating. And reflecting. The years
go by. Verrrrry slooowwly. Finally, at the age of forty and during the
month of Ramadan, Muhammad receives a revelation from God.
A few years later, he leaves the cave and begins proclaiming God's
message. He also proclaims that he is no longer just that loner dude
from the cave but a prophet of God along the lines of Abraham,
Moses, and Jesus. He invites his followers to surrender—*islam,* in
Arabic—to God. He gains followers, and by the time Muhammad
dies in 632, most of the Arab peninsula has converted to his teachings. These include a variety of familiar takes on the afterlife, like
immortal souls, Judgment-Day resurrection, and a dualistic paradise (Jannah) and hell (Jahannam). Peppered into these doctrines,
however, are some less familiar details. Like how paradise isn't just a

spiritually pleasurable place but a physically sweet one, too, thanks to a bunch of nubile, virginal *houri*s assigned to its male residents. And how hellgoers will be forced to eat the demon-headed fruit of the evil tree Zaqqum, which will then make them really thirsty—but the only drink on tap at Club Jahannam is boiling water. Which is rarely known for its thirst-quenching qualities.[12]

THIRTEENTH CENTURY, PERU

The Incan empire rises to prominence among the lush Peruvian highlands. Unfortunately, this prominence only lasts a couple of centuries, because eventually Spanish conquistadors show up at the helm of their fancy boats while wearing their fancy pants-and-armor gear and bearing fancy weapons technology. Then they devastate all the indigenous peoples with fancy strains of smallpox. New World: *conquered*.

Anyway, prior to dying out in droves, the Incas believe in a dualistic afterlife. On the bad side, people end up in a frozen, torturous, underground realm where they're forced to eat rocks. Even worse, their dining companions are probably all those disease-bearing Spaniards. On the positive side, good Incas go to a heavenly realm in the presence of the sun god, Inti. So, smallpox notwithstanding, it's not such a bad thing when a good Inca dies. Unless that good, dead Inca is a king. Why? Because the king's wives and servants and advisors are expected to follow him in death. Willingly. Keep that in mind, kids, when filling out your Incan palace job application. It's not expressly stated, but "other tasks as needed" may include suicide.

---

12. Lots more about the heaven and hell of Islam in Chapter 4.

1308–1321, ITALY

Dante didn't give his work the title *Divine comedy*. He called it, simply, *commedia*. (He was Italian, after all.) Giovanni Boccaccio later referred to it by adding the "Divina," and the nickname stuck.

Famed Italian poet Dante Alighieri writes his masterwork, the *Divine Comedy*. But don't let the name fool you. It's not really that funny, unless you get your yippies from scenes of torture. Dante's allegorical epic describes what happens to human souls once they slip the surly bonds of regular life and fly headlong into the afterlife. In the story, the central character—Dante himself—gets guided by the poet Virgil through hell, purgatory, and heaven. Each destination has its own section in the poem, called *Inferno* (hell), *Purgatorio* (purgatory), and *Paradiso* (heaven).

Unless Dante was a raging egotist, he likely had no idea how crazy influential his poem would be. Many of his details wedge themselves into the public consciousness, from the sign on hell's gate ("Abandon all hope, ye who enter here") to the horrible-but-fitting punishments in the nine subterranean circles of hell (blasphemers lie captive in a flaming desert, beneath a rain of fire) to the indescribable glories of heaven.[13] In fact, some commentators have suggested that the popular Christian idea of hell as a place where sinners suffer conscious torment owes more to Dante than the New Testament. Try to keep that opinion to yourself, though. No self-respecting fiery evangelist

---

13. See pp. 185–186 and pp. 188–189 for more about Dante and the creative punishments of hell and purgatory.

wants to know his sweaty, fire-and-brimstone approach to soul-winning has its roots in prissy Italian poetry.

FOURTEENTH CENTURY, CENTRAL MEXICO

The Aztecs achieve cultural, political, and military dominance over what is now considered Central America. More than their Mayan predecessors and Incan contemporaries to the south, the Aztecs have a wonderfully detailed set of afterlife beliefs. Their post-death landscape contains no less than four different realms: a celestial paradise for male warriors and victims of human sacrifice (and apparently, there are a ghastly number of these); a celestial paradise for women who die in childbirth; a southern paradise for people who die of causes related to the water-god Tlaloc (like death via lightning strike or drowning); and a hellish realm of the dead called Mictlan. Most people end up in Mictlan, which is a real downer. Dying, of course, is bad enough. But the Mictlan-bound have to die and then pack their afterlife bags for a harrowing roadtrip through nine levels of the underworld.[14] Rest up before you rest in peace.

1415, WESTERN EUROPE

The first of two Latin texts called the *Ars Moriendi* ("The Art of Dying") makes its first appearance across Western Europe, on the heels of the Black Death and The Hundred Years' War between France and England. You know what they say about war and pestilence: they make people think about death. Which turned these fun little

---

14. You can read more about these four destinations in Chapter 4. Unless you skipped ahead. If so, stop it. Sheesh.

handbooks (the shorter, second text was written in 1540) into insanely successful runaway best sellers.[15] They include practical advice on how to die a good, Christian death. Topics include what to expect during the death process, temptations to avoid upon dying, how to make sure your salvation stays intact during death, and how friends and family should care for the dying.

The second text is especially interesting, thanks to its many illustrations, a few of which graphically illustrate what happens in the spiritual world at the time of death. Hint: It's a lot. For instance, when a person dies, apparently a tiny little body-shaped soul tries to escape through the mouth of the deceased. It's guarded by an angel. And that's a good thing, because at the same time a skeletal Death and horned Satan are trying to capture it for their own devious purposes.

The original handbooks led to a long tradition of Catholic *Ars Moriendi* texts, produced over the next two centuries to help people die well. Or, at least, to give them a frightening mental image of the spiritual tussle between angels and demons that's occurring RIGHT NEXT TO THEIR DEATH BED. Shiver.

1510, THE NETHERLANDS

The Dutch painter—and devout Catholic—Hieronymus Bosch paints his famous triptych, *Paradise and Hell,* which is full of the kind of nightmare-inducing afterlife imagery that rivals Dante in terms of influence. Bosch's depiction of hell is particularly graphic. It's a fiery place (natch), occupied by demonic half-human/half-machine

---

15. Sounds impressive, until you consider that both books were some of the first mass-printed books in history, thanks to Gutenberg.

creatures charged with inflicting agony on sinful souls. Which is a bold thing to paint in the early years of the sixteenth century. These Transformers from hell very seriously freak people out. So, naturally, the freaked-out public accuses Bosch of being a Satan-worshipper. On account of his willingness to use his Christian imagination to describe hell.

The *Pocket Guide* asks that you do not jump to that conclusion in response to the contents of this book.

1510, WEST AFRICA

The slave trade begins. The *Pocket Guide* is reluctant to say anything positive about this history-shaping development, though it does have one notable effect for our purposes: It ships the beliefs and ritual practices of the areas surrounding the Gulf of Guinea across the Atlantic to the Americas. One of these religious traditions is Vodun or Voudou, a multi-deity, ancestor-based affair that ends up modifying some elements of Catholicism on its way to becoming Voodoo, the folk religion now practiced in Haiti, Jamaica, the Dominican Republic, Louisiana, and a few other places.

Thanks to Hollywood, Voodoo suffers from a variety of wild (and alarmist) misrepresentations like attaching it to voodoo dolls, devil worship, and violent bloody rituals. But as far as religions go, it does have a few oddities. Such as spirit possession being a *good* thing. Then there's the Voodoo death ceremony, called *dessounin,* in which a priest separates the person's *gros-bon-ange* (the part of the soul that contains the life force) from the body and boots it into the cosmos, where it turns into a helpful ancestral spirit. Sounds easy, but if the priest screws up and accidentally separates the deceased's *ti-bon-ange* (the part of the soul that contains the personality and characteristics) from the body, it could turn evil, possess innocent bystanders, or make the corpse susceptible to being turned into a zombie by a dark sorcerer called a *bokor*. Accidental zombification is a real good way to ruin a perfectly decent death ritual.

1545–1563, ITALY

The nineteenth Ecumenical Council of the Roman Catholic Church convenes in Trent, over three different periods, to hammer out a variety of doctrines in response to the charges of the Protestant Reformation. Among other proclamations, it decrees during the twenty-fifth session that contrary to the teachings of that annoying jerk Luther, Purgatory *does* in fact exist, and that souls residing therein are detained there until they have been cleaned up and made fit for heaven. And if a bunch of old white guys declare it, then that settles it. Nanny-nanny-boo-boo, Marty Boy.

CHAPTER 3

Great Moments in Eternity, Part 2

(A Timeline: 1743 to Present Day)

The eighteenth century kicked off a period that became known as the Age of Enlightenment. It was an exciting time. People got really keyed up about things like reason, and rationalism, and intellectual progress. No longer did we need ancient pagan superstitions or tired old religious traditions. Now we had newfangled stuff like science, and industry, and democracy. And America! Good times indeed.

You'd think this would lead to a decline in our fascination with unknowable concepts like the soul and our eternal destiny. But you'd be wrong. If anything, it led to more speculation. And more kooky characters. And way, way, *way* more attempts to communicate with dead people.

That's good news for the *Pocket Guide*. Thanks, Enlightenment!

1743, SWEDEN

A scientist and inventor named Emanuel Swedenborg begins having a series of craaaazy dreams. Some are sexual. Some are horrifying. But almost all of them involve encounters with the likes of Jesus, God, guardian angels, historical figures, and other elements of the mystical realm. But they're not just dreams. They're . . . *real*. These dreams last until 1744 and have such a profound effect on Swedenborg that he decides to pursue the supernatural dreamworld full-time. He abandons his regular job to become a professional spiritual commentator, paranormal messenger, and all-around oddball.

Before long, he's regularly lapsing into self-induced states of ecstasy in order to receive communications from the spirit world. He gains street cred by making a few oddly accurate psychic outbursts. He painstakingly describes his travels to other dimensions, including heaven and hell, both of which he says are much like regular life—people have jobs, get married, pursue leisure, go to war—only lots nicer or lots worse. Depending, of course, whether your final destination will be smoking or nonsmoking.

Swedenborg's friends think he's gone wacko, but the sentiment isn't universal. By the end of the century, Swedenborgian Christian churches are being founded in Europe and the United States, based on his theology.[1] And everyone from the spiritualists of the nineteenth century to literary greats like William Blake, Samuel Coleridge, and Ralph Waldo Emerson end up claiming him as a profound influence.

---

1. Some are still active today, with congregations across North America (www. swedenborg.com). Famous Swedenborgians include spiritual luminaries like Johnny Appleseed and Helen Keller.

1779, PARIS

A German scientist and physician named Franz Anton Mesmer kicks off the spiritualism movement by publishing an eighty-eight-page booklet that introduces "*magnétisme animal*" (animal magnetism) to the unsuspecting public.

Somehow Mesmer comes to the conclusion that a magnetic fluid surrounds all living things and influences them in the same way a magnet influences metal. Thus, animal magnetism. It's kind of like the Force, but with magnets instead of lightsabers.

Mesmerize (v.): to fascinate, hold spellbound, or metaphorically hypnotize.

So sickness, Mesmer says, is the result of that fluid being blocked as it attempts to flow through the body. But don't despair. Mesmer designs a special kind of massage technique that helps the body return to harmony with all that blocked-up fluid. In a genius marketing move, he gives the technique a catchy name: *mesmerizing*.

Only the mesmerizing process comes with an unintended side effect. Mesmer's massages tend to put his clients into a trance-like sleep. And these sleepytimes can be unpredictable. Weird stuff allegedly starts to happen—like contact with the dead, who seemingly use this so-called fluid as a telephone from The Beyond. *Ooooh,* his French audiences realize, *hypnotized people can talk to spirits! Fantastique!* So they get really into it. Spiritualism is born. Psychics come out of the woodwork. Séances become the rage. Ghosts appear in every old house in the Western hemisphere. And for his trouble, Mesmer gets a word named after him.

1805, EASTERN INDIANA

An alcoholic Shawnee medicine man named Tenskwatawa—the consonant-rich brother of Tecumsah—lapses into a coma during an epidemic. His tribesmen think he's dead. They start preparing for the funeral. Then, in what must have been a hilariously sitcom-ish scene, Tenskwatawa wakes up all crazy-eyed, claiming to have just taken an out-of-body-style trip through heaven and hell. Heaven? A fertile hunting ground with lots of fish, game, and corn fields. Hell? A place where naughty Shawnee are forced to drink molten lead and experience other tortures. In time, additional revelations follow, only without the near-death drama. Tenskwatawa spins his newfound mojo into a career as an important prophet and Shawnee leader. His central message—that white Americans are the spawn of Satan—ends up being extraordinarily popular among Native Americans. Not sure why.

1823, NEW ENGLAND

A failed farmer named Joseph Smith claims to have received a visit from an angel/resurrected prophet named Moroni, who reveals to him the existence and whereabouts of a buried book written on gold plates. Four years later, Smith digs up the plates and suddenly discovers he's been given the gift of a lifetime: a direct line to God the Father and Jesus Christ his Son. The plates are in a weird pictographic language, but this is no problem for a resourceful ex-farmer. Smith simply dials up his holy decoder ring, figures out the language is "Reformed Egyptian," and translates the plates into English. The result? The Book of Mormon.

Smitty then gets busy restoring a true church made of true believers. They call themselves the Latter-Day Saints. And it's good to be a latter-day saint, Smith says, because in those latter days they'll reign with Jesus in the world to come. And by "reign" he means ruling and repopulating an extraterrestrial planet with your spirit family in the Mormon afterlife.[2] Meanwhile, Joe goes through some challenging years. He gets married, oh, several dozen times. He gets tarred and feathered once or twice. He ends up in jail on multiple occasions. Eventually, in 1844, he's murdered by an angry throng of anti-Mormon militiamen.[3] Let this be a lesson to any of you thinking of founding a new American religion.

1848, NEW YORK

Two teenage sisters in Hydesville, New York, throw fuel on the fire Mesmer built when they claim the ability to communicate with a ghost who haunts their parents' house. It seems Katie and Maggie Fox have been getting tapping messages—in a convenient alphabetical code—from a dead guy named Charles Rosa. Poor Charles explains to them he was a peddler who'd gotten himself murdered in the house and buried in the cellar, long before the Fox family ever moved in. Assuming ghosts to be generally trustworthy sources, reporters jump on the story and turn the Fox girls into media sensations. Sweet.

---

2. No lie. Learn more on p. 98 in the next chapter.

3. It's been speculated that some of these militiamen were former followers of Smith who were upset because he kept trying to steal their wives for his own polygamist purposes.

It gets even sweeter when P.T. Barnum shows up. He signs a contract with the Fox sisters and takes their happy, tappy, talk-to-the-dead show on the road. But the showbiz life ends up the death of them. The sisters eventually become alcoholics. They battle regular accusations of fraud. In 1888, Maggie admits to faking the on-stage séances and rapping noises. How? With toe-cracking. *Spooky* toe-cracking. And there's more: After the sisters die in the early 1890s, investigators dig up the cellar of the girls' childhood home and discover a buried skeleton. "Charles Rosa lives!" say the true believers. "The bones were planted!" say the skeptics. The Fox sisters, unexpectedly, are unavailable for comment. Even via toe-cracking.

1856, FRANCE

A doctor with the ridiculously French name Hippolyte Leon Denizard Rivail publishes *The Book of the Spirits* under the pseudonym Allan Kardec. The pen name is a good choice. Anyway, Kardec had previously discovered that he had the ability to enter into a hypnotic trance and produce a whole lot of writing, despite not being fully conscious. Notably, most of that writing had to do with his long history of reincarnation.[4]

As *The Book of the Spirits* and his other writings begin to draw attention, Kardec hits the lecture circuit. He teaches that reincarnation is necessary for humans to progress spiritually. But it's not all kittens and daisies, because some past incarnations can actually be negative. And these downer past lives can cause trouble in the present one, in the form of psychological problems like schizophrenia, multiple

---

4. By the way, he got the pseudonym from personal revelations that two of his names in past lives were Allan and Kardec.

personality disorders, and even epilepsy. So people ought to try to understand their past lives, he says, in order to get better. Guess what? That sounds a whole lot like past-life therapy, which doesn't become popular until more than a hundred years later.[5] Seems for all his super-lengthy past, Kardec knows something about the future, too.

1862, NEW ENGLAND

John Nelson Darby, an Irish evangelist and preacher, arrives in America for the first of several missionary tours. The originator of the Plymouth Brethren movement, Darby preaches a Christian theological framework called *dispensationalism,* which is way too complicated to explain here and still maintain the pocket-sized nature of this book. Suffice it to say, it places a great deal of focus on the End Times and is directly responsible for, among other things, (1) a literal interpretation of the New Testament book of Revelation as a blueprint for future events, including believers' hope for a glorious heaven and Satan's being cast into a fiery hell; (2) Christian support for the nation of Israel; (3) the best-selling *Left Behind* series of novels; and (4) the continued film career of child actor Kirk Cameron.[6]

1867, NEW YORK

A clairvoyant named Andrew Jackson Davis—who, surprisingly, has little to do with the Confederacy (or, for that matter, Kirk Cameron)—publishes *A Stellar Key to the Summer Land.* Its purpose,

---

5. See the 1978 entry on p. 88.
6. For more on dispensationalism, you'll want to read *Pocket Guide to the Apocalypse: The Official Field Manual for the End of the World* (Relevant Books, 2005).

In 1844, Andrew Jackson Davis claimed to have been magically transported forty miles away into the Catskill Mountains, where he hung out briefly with no less than famous philosopher-mystic Emanuel Swedenborg and Galen, the ancient Greek physician. At the time, both Swedenborg and the Doc were pretty seriously dead. So there's proof of his "substantial existence after death" right there.

he writes, is to "furnish scientific and philosophical evidences of an inhabitable sphere or zone among the suns and planets of space . . . to all who seek a solid, rational, philosophical foundation on which to rest their hopes of a substantial existence after death."[7] Most of that evidence comes from his having personally gazed upon an otherworldly realm called, in fact, the "Summer Land." It's way more than just a nice, warm, sunshiny place. It's the highest level of the afterlife humans can enter.

And he hasn't just seen it, AJD claims. He can actually go there any time he darn well pleases, slipping into and out of the spirit realm at will. So naturally he offers himself as a font of information about what happens to the soul after death. Because he's totally been there.

1882, LONDON

English physicist Sir William Barrett and journalist/spiritualist Edmund Dawson Rogers found the Society for Psychical Research. Why? Because they're into ghost investigations, telepathy, trance

---

7. From the explanatory preface to the 1868 printing. Davis, Andrew Jackson. *Stellar Key to the Summer Land* (Boston: William White & Company, 1868).

states, and other uncanny topics, but the rest of the guys at the pub just couldn't be bothered by any of it. So Barrett and Rogers start a club based upon their shared interests.

Then they merge with another club. In an exemplary marriage of kooks, the SPR joins forces with the famed Sidgwick Group, led by well-respected Cambridge philosophy professor Henry Sidgwick. The combined Dream Team of paranormal investigators goes on to expose frauds, experience unexplainable phenomena, publish thousands of articles, and produce one awesomely titled book, *Phantasm of the Living,* in 1886. You will be delighted to know the Society for Psychical Research is still active today. In this realm for sure (www.spr.ac.uk). Probably in others, too.

1890, AMERICAN WEST

A Native American religious movement called the Ghost Dance sweeps the nation. It starts with the Paiute people of Nevada, who are led by a prophet/shaman known as either Wovoka or Jack Wilson, depending on the crowd.[8] And like Tenskwatawa decades earlier, Wovoka has another one of those trance-like visions where everyone thinks he's dead, but then *He! Wakes! Up! Having received a message! From God!* Moses had his burning bush. Native Americans have their not-dead-yet pseudo resurrections.

Anyway, during his trance, Wovoka visits heaven and downloads a step-by-step guide to the Ghost Dance, a five-day ritual that's

---

8. Wovoka (Paiute for "wood cutter") was orphaned as a child and raised by a white Christian rancher named David Wilson. But no self-respecting Native American shaman wants a mayonnaise Anglo name like "Jack Wilson," so the *Pocket Guide* totally understands the choice to go with the stage name.

supposed to rid the world of evil, renew humanity with peace and prosperity, and hasten the day when the living would be reunited with their departed ancestors.[9]

Nationwide, tribes adopt the Ghost Dance. The main draw is the part where, around Day 4, participants get all hypnotized by the rhythmic swaying and dazed by the lack of sleep and fall into a trance—at which point they're supposed to hear from dead relatives. Unfortunately, the dance doesn't just capture the attention of the tribes. Or their dead relatives. Nope, the U.S. military antennae go up. They get the notion that (gasp!) this religious movement could lead to a violent uprising. So they conduct a violent uprising of their own. On December 29, 1890, American troops massacre three hundred nonviolent Sioux ghost dancers at Wounded Knee.

1893, CHICAGO

These are dark days for spiritualism. Accusations of fakery are flying. Spirit communicators are admitting to fraud. What's a person with an authentic connection to another realm to do? A couple of Unitarian ministers answer this question by joining up with medium/ author Cora L. Richmond to form a bureaucracy: the National Spiritualist Association of Churches (NSAC). It's an attempt to establish some standards for ordained Spiritualist ministers. The association operates with an intriguingly church-like hierarchical structure, ripe with state associations and an annual convention and interpersonal squabbling (sample issues: *Is it OK to believe in reincarnation? Are Spiritualists Christians? Was Jesus the Son of God or just an*

---

9. Impressive dance-related outcome. Too bad you can't say the same for the tango.

awesome medium? When is it acceptable to blame passed gas on a ghost's ectoplasmic aroma?) Eventually, the NSAC adopts a Declaration of Principles. Among its articles are "We affirm that the existence and personal identity of the individual continue after the change called death" and "We affirm that communication with the so-called dead is a fact, scientifically proven by the phenomena of Spiritualism." The so-called dead rejoice from the beyond, because now their disembodied voices can be heard.

1901, BALTIMORE

Businessman William Fuld begins manufacturing and selling the first mass-produced ouija boards, in which a planchette mysteriously points to letters or words in response to questions. At long last, contact with the spirit world is made available to every American, psychic or not. Looking for hours of nonstop family fun? Why not try to communicate with the dead?

As one might expect, reactions are mixed. For every hour of nonstop family fun, there are groups criticizing ouija boards for bringing unsuspecting children into contact with demons. Other charges include the tendency of ouija boards to inspire suicide, induce insanity, and create really bad poetry.

An estimated 20 million ouija boards have been sold in the United States and Europe over the past forty years.

1910, NEW HAMPSHIRE

Famed American psychologist and philosopher William James dies at the age of sixty-eight. This is an important moment in the history of the afterlife, as it allows a horde of mediums to maintain meaningful work. Because William James isn't just famous; he's well-respected, too. He was a legitimate scientist. He was the author of important books like *The Varieties of Religious Experience*. And even though he had a more-than-passing interest in spiritualism and life after death, the dude was a long, long way from being a crackpot.

So, when James dies, his posthumous popularity soars among those claiming to provide knowledge from beyond the grave, because suddenly all that knowledge is apparently coming from him. Ghost-whisperers keep pestering his departed spirit during séances. Several mediums announce he has appeared to them in bodily form. His ghost (allegedly) shows up in a variety of convenient places. The attraction of this is obvious, because who would you trust more? A rapping murdered peddler like the Fox sisters' Charles Rosa? Or a genius researcher like William James?

1923, TEXAS

A former Disciples of Christ Sunday school teacher named Edgar Cayce begins to give regular psychic readings while subjected to that old standby—the hypnosis-induced trance. This allows him to unconsciously prescribe cures to sick people. Which is a nice thing to do. But before long, Cayce's simple cures morph into esoteric discussions of past lives and reincarnation. This is, um, a little awkward for Cayce. Because Sunday school teachers don't normally advocate that kind of stuff, unconscious or not. But what can you do?

Over the next several years, Cayce lets it flow. He performs some fourteen thousand of these readings, many of which are recorded and published after his death in 1945. His posthumous teachings on reincarnation blow up in the 1960s and '70s, leading to widespread public interest in the subject of past lives.[10] Cayce gains more fame in the grave than he ever got while alive, which means the dude had (ahem) a pretty successful life after death.

1924, UNITED STATES

Arthur Augustus Ford, a former Disciples of Christ preacher, steals a page out of the Edgar Cayce handbook. While in a trance, he receives revelations from someone named Fletcher, a supposedly French-Canadian friend of his who died during World War I. People dig it, so Ford takes Fletcher public. Presumably, Fletcher agrees to this plan—his schedule is pretty flexible, on account of how he exists outside time and space—so the two of them team up to deliver messages from the dead to freaked-out audiences worldwide.

One of the most famous messages from Fletcher is (allegedly) a secret code from the late Harry Houdini to Houdini's wife, Bess, which the Houdinis had arranged before his death in order to satisfy their curiosity about the afterlife. According to reports, Ford reveals the code, and Bess confirms that it's correct. Score one

---

10. It didn't hurt that he located most of his clients' past lives in cool places like the lost world of Atlantis and Revolutionary War–era United States. Very few seemed to have been around during the bubonic plague or grown up as feudal serfs.

for spiritualism. But wait: A few years later, Bess denies that Ford cracked the code.[11]

So did he or didn't he? And is Fletcher for real? No one ever finds out one way or another. The truth is hard to get at when it's bundled in a straitjacket and suspended in a Chinese water torture cell.

1930, ENGLAND

Three research buddies make a pact: Whichever one of them dies first will try to get in touch with the other two from behind the veil, thus proving the possibility of life after death. It's a brilliant plan. Also kind of dorky. The three spiritualists—George Jobson, A. J. Ashdown, and B. K. Kirkby—devise a secret message for the newly deceased to send. It's Kirkby's initials: *B.K.K.*

Poor Jobson is the first of the trio to kick the bucket. He dies in 1930. But he fails to follow the rules. Sure, he sends the code (allegedly) three months after dying. But he mistakenly sends it to the wrong person. That's right: Some random, unknown medium claims to have received the secret signal. (In Jobson's defense, the afterlife *can* be confusing.) However, the botched message intrigues the two remaining friends, who immediately get to work trying to track down Old Dead Jobson. To make the task easier, Ashdown and Kirkby form the Ashkir-Jobson Trianion. Their mission? To develop mechanical devices to communicate with the dead. So they commence developing. Among their inventions are the Reflectograph

---

11. You want to know what the code was, don't you? Supposedly, it was a single word: *Believe.*

(a special typewriter for ghosts), the Communigraph (a pendulum-based spiritual communications device), and the Ashkir-Jobson Vibrator (a device that is so *not* what you think it is, you sick sick sicko; it's a tuning fork used in séances).

In their case, necessity isn't exactly the mother of invention. No, necessity is invention's old dead friend.

1944, SWITZERLAND

Carl Gustav Jung, the world-renowned Swiss psychologist and founder of analytical psychology, suffers a heart attack after being hospitalized for breaking his foot. This leads to his own near-death experience—complete with an accompanying "bright glow"—during which he remembers rising far above the earth into space. He describes this experience, along with the appearance of the world from this height, in surprising detail in an autobiography called *Memories, Dreams, Reflections.*[12] Jung clings to this memory as he ages and becomes fascinated with ideas of the afterlife. Based on the existence of death dreams and myths, he concludes that—whether or not survival after death is actually possible—the psyche behaves *as if* it is true. Subconsciously, all of us expect to pass into some sort of awareness in the afterlife. Which means death should be joyful, not catastrophic. Jung gets to test the accuracy of this idea when he dies in 1961.

---

12. It was written between 1957 and 1961, when Jung died, several years before the first photographic images of the earth from space. See Jung, C.G. *Memories, Dreams, Reflections,* Aniela Jaffe, ed., and Richard and Clara Winston, trans. (New York: Random House, 1961).

1947, CLEVELAND

Claude Beck, a professor of surgery at Case Western Reserve University Medical School in Cleveland, uses a defibrillator for the first time to revive a stopped human heart. It occurs during an operation on a fourteen-year-old boy. Beck jolts the heart muscle with electricity from the defibrillator and, *shazam!* it restores the heart's rhythm.

So what? you are probably thinking. *Big heart-shocking deal.* But what you don't know is that, as medical use of the defibrillator increases over the next few decades, so do the accounts of near-death experiences. Which makes sense. If you can't resuscitate that heart attack victim, then he can't wake up and tell you about the bright lights and soothing voices of the afterlife.[13] Thanks, Dr. Beck!

1950, UNITED STATES

A science fiction author named Lafayette Ronald "L. Ron" Hubbard publishes a book called *Dianetics: The Modern Science of Mental Health*.[14] It becomes a runaway best seller, introducing unsuspecting readers to Hubbard's belief that the mind is split into two parts: the conscious analytical mind and the unconscious "reactive mind." The reactive mind, he says, records every perception it ever receives. This means it remembers everything that ever happened to you—even the stuff that occurred in earlier lifetimes. A *lot* of earlier lifetimes.

---

13. For additional near-death fun, see the 1977 entry on p. 87.
14. Hubbard, L. Ron. *Dianetics: The Modern Science of Mental Health* (Los Angeles: The American Saint Hill Organization, 1950).

Because L. Ron believes some people have been around for gazillions of years. The Dianetics process—along with Scientology, the system of beliefs and practices that emerge from it—involves cleaning out all these unwanted recordings in the brain, then filling the space with better stuff. Which might include, say, the Scientology origins story about an alien warrior who brought a bunch of regular alien folk to earth millions of years ago in alien spaceships, only to blow the poor aliens to pieces, leaving their disembodied alien souls floating around waiting to attach to human bodies—and *boy,* does the presence of these space ghosts mess with our heads. Proof? Tom Cruise.

According to F.A.C.T.Net, Inc. (the Fight Against Coercive Tactics Network, www.factnet.org), the turnover rate for Scientology is around 95 percent every three to five years. Which means, of the estimated 8 million people who've entered the program since Hubbard started it up, 7.95 million of them are no longer involved. So apparently it takes three to five years before they fill you in on the alien stuff.

1952, COLORADO

An amateur hypnotist named Morey Bernstein tells Virginia Tighe, a housewife from Pueblo, that she's getting very, very sleepy. As she enters a trance, Bernstein puts Virginia through a process called hypnotic regression, hoping she'll revert to her childhood. But Virginia

81

overachieves a little in the reversion, skipping right past childhood and into a past life as a nineteenth-century Irishwoman named Bridey Murphy. It seems Bridey grew up in the village of Cork and died from a fall. As Bridey, Virginia describes life in nineteenth-century Ireland in fascinating detail (and with a believable Irish brogue). This is unexpected, since Tighe wasn't born until 1923 and had never been to Ireland. The whole weird story gains national media attention in 1956 when Bernstein writes a best-selling book about it, *The Search for Bridey Murphy*.[15] Skeptical investigators eventually uncover a few problematic facts—as a child, Tighe lived across the street from an Irish immigrant named, um, Bridie Murphey, which means her memories of Ireland may well have come from childhood memories of her neighbor *telling* about Ireland—but nevertheless, her story leads to the reincarnation publishing boom of the mid-twentieth century.[16]

1960, VIRGINIA

Speaking of reincarnation, a Canadian-American medical doctor, psychiatrist, and psychic researcher named Ian Stevenson lends his significant—and legitimate—academic credentials to paranormal studies with the publication of an article called "The Evidence for Survival from Claimed Memories of Former Incarnations" in the *Journal of the American Society for Psychical Research*. The article reports on his study of 2,500 cases of individuals claiming to have experienced multiple lives. Unlike most paranormal investigators,

---

15. Bernstein, Morey. *The Search for Bridey Murphy* (New York: Doubleday, 1956).
16. It also kick-starts the past-life therapy craze of the 1980s. Check out the 1978 entry a few pages to the right.

his research is academically stringent and, if not accepted, at least cautiously respected by the scholarly world. Stevenson goes on to publish several books for the scientific community, including *Twenty Cases Suggestive of Reincarnation* (1966) and *Children Who Remember Previous Lives: A Question of Reincarnation* (1987),[17] in which he interviews young children from around the world who seem to be able describe their past lives (and deaths) in considerable detail. He is gracious enough not to describe these children as completely creepy. But it's implied.

1962, MICHIGAN

A college physics teacher named Robert C. W. Ettinger self-publishes *The Prospect of Immortality,* in which he proposes refrigeration as a novel way to survive death. His idea? Freeze people immediately after they expire, then resuscitate them in the future when mankind knows a whole lot more about . . . defrosting. The book is republished in 1964 by Doubleday, and suddenly cryonics—the practice of deep-freezing a corpse for preservation and future revival—becomes a legitimate afterlife option for wide-eyed optimists, and not just Ice Age cavemen. Also aboard the cryonics train? Hall of Fame ballplayer Ted Williams.[18] As of the publication of this *Pocket Guide,* there are several current organizations that will freeze your body (or, for a reduced rate, just your head) and keep it chilled until the tissue-repairing nano-technology is advanced enough to bring you back. The six-figure fee

---

17. Stevenson, Ian. *Twenty Cases Suggestive of Reincarnation* (Charlottesville: University Press of Virginia, 1966) and *Children Who Remember Previous Lives: A Question of Reincarnation* (Jefferson, NC: McFarland Press, 1987).

18. But not Walt Disney. He was cremated, which is pretty much the exact opposite of cryonics. The frozen-Disney story is an urban legend.

is totally worth it. Especially for Star Wars fans who geek out on the whole Han Solo–carbonite plot.

1967, ENGLAND

Dame Cicely Saunders, an Anglican doctor and nurse, founds St. Christopher's in southeast London, the world's first hospice built to allow the terminally ill to die with dignity and a minimum amount of pain and discomfort. Dr. Saunders believes that dying is a natural event and that the transition from this world to the next should be life-affirming rather than scary, an opportunity for gratitude and happiness rather than pain. Her influence earns her a variety of awards and honors, and in most respects, Dr. Saunders creates the entire hospice movement in contemporary medicine. She dies of cancer in 2005, at the age of eighty-seven. She spends the final days of her life at St. Christopher's.

1968, SWEDEN

Konstantin Raudive, a Latvian philosopher and psychologist at a Swedish university, publishes a book, in German, called *The Inaudible Made Audible.* In it, he details his research into Electronic Voice Phenomenon, the supposed practice of electronically recording the voices of departed spirits. Raudive, it seems, has recorded some 100,000 snippets of disembodied people making noise.[19] Sometimes

---

19. Wanna capture your own EVP? You can do it at home. Find a tape or digital recorder. Hit "record." Ask open-ended questions, like "Am I talking to a dead person?" or "Do you like my shirt?" Then just sit there. After a long time, hit "Stop." Rewind and listen again. Turn up the volume. Does any of the hissing or static sound like the ghostly answers to your questions? Congratulations! Listen real hard and try to figure out what's being said.

they use identifiable phrases or words. Sometimes they mix languages within a single sentence. Sometimes the sound is just weird scratchy stuff that must obviously be a secret ghost code. (Unfortunately, none of these recordings contain a voice saying "Boo!" or the sound of chains being dragged across the ceiling.) In 1971, Raudive's book gets translated into English. It's called *Breakthrough: An Amazing Experiment in Electronic Communication with the Dead*. And from that point on, any examples of electronic voice phenomena come to be known as Raudive Voices. Breakthrough, indeed.

1971, VIRGINIA

An advertising exec named Robert Monroe introduces the phrase "out-of-body-experience" to the vernacular with the publication of a book called *Journeys: Out of the Body*.[20] It tells of his experiences, beginning in 1958, of traveling outside his body while maintaining full consciousness. He induces these experiments by a variety of methods that include (but are not limited to) huffing chemicals and/or self-hypnosis. He goes on to research out-of-body experiences and claims to have cultivated the ability to slip from this dimension into another dimension. This dimension-slipping includes a trip to the post-death realm, where he hangs out for awhile with his deceased father. Later, Monroe founds a big cable company in central Virginia. But that's neither here nor there.[21]

---

20. Monroe, Robert A. *Journeys: Out of the Body* (New York: Doubleday, 1971).

21. Actually, it is there. In Virginia. Unless you actually live in central Virginia, in which case it's here. So on second thought, the cable company thing is *both* here and there. Dang. The *Pocket Guide* regrets the error.

1976, TENNESSEE

A Chattanooga housewife named Mary K. Baxter meets up with Jesus one night, who tells her that God has a special plan for her: it's to see both heaven and hell and then to write about what she sees. So Jesus separates Mary's spirit from her body and escorts her into hell every night for thirty nights in a row. Then Mary and Jesus tour heaven for ten straight nights. Then she writes the books *A Divine Revelation of Hell* (1993) and *A Divine Revelation of Heaven* (1998).[22]

One of her most divine revelations is that most of the spirits in hell look like skeletons with ragged, wormy flesh. And people are literally being burned in pits. But heaven's a lot nicer. It's filled with flying angels and worshipful white horses and literal crowns for its residents to wear and even rooms of unclaimed blessings. Which, for heaven, seems a bit of a downer. But anyway, Mary is eventually ordained as a Pentecostal minister and her books sell bajillions of copies. Ain't nobody gonna accuse her of not claiming her blessings.

1977, WASHINGTON STATE

A 35,000-year-old warlord from the days of Atlantis "appears" to Judith Darlene Hampton and her husband in the kitchen of their trailer in Tacoma. The warrior's name is Ramtha, and he's not just a man of action. He's philosophical, too. In fact, he tells Judith that he's responsible for most of the great teachings of Socrates *and* Hinduism, among other beliefs. This is exceedingly good news for

---

22. Baxter, Mary K. *A Divine Revelation of Hell* (New Kensington, PA: Whitaker House, 1993) and *A Divine Revelation of Heaven* (New Kensington, PA: Whitaker House, 1998).

the Hamptons, because ten years later, Judith—now going by the stage name J. Z. Knight—piggybacks off Ramtha for significant personal gain. She trademarks his name and teachings, channels him for national television audiences (her voice gets deeper and she speaks with a weird accent), begins publishing books, and performs a ribbon-cutting at the Ramtha School for Enlightenment. Knight's conferences on channeling, consciousness, and reincarnation attract thousands who pay to hear from the ancient superhero philosopher. There's a valuable lesson here, kids: Wanna be rich and famous? Find some old dead guy from a theoretical lost world to speak New Age platitudes through you. Works every time.

1977, UNITED STATES AND INDIA

Two Icelandic scientists named Karlis Osis and Erlendur Haraldsson publish a book called *At the Hour of Death,* which summarizes a four-year study of the deathbed experiences of fifty thousand terminally ill patients in the United States and India. They pay particular attention to people who keep their wits about them until the final breath, because who better to describe the metaphysics of what's happening than a nearly dead chatterbox?

The big reveal: Regardless of culture, age, class, gender, religion, or socio-economic status, all the death-bed testimonies are weirdly similar. Patients describe feelings of peace and happiness. They tell of the presence of light or intense color. Best of all, they report an awareness of really and truly being in an otherworldly place. So either everyone's headed to the same heavenly destination, or hell's greeters have replaced those "Abandon all hope . . ." billboards with a complex system of bright lights and mystical mood enhancers. No need to cause unnecessary dismay. At least not yet.

1978, UNITED STATES

Thanks to Bridey Murphy and J. Z. Knight and the public's growing fascination with reincarnation, three books hit U.S. shelves in the same year, all having to do with hypnotic regression and past-life therapy. *Reliving Past Lives* (by Helen Wambach), *You Have Been Here Before* (by Edith Fiore), and *Past Lives Therapy* (by Morris Netherton) each discuss dealing with physical and emotional problems by exploring trauma that probably was caused from past incarnations.[23] Which means most people went through the 1980s needing to be hypnotized so they could manage their carryover phobias and allergies and psychological troubles. This is great news, because suddenly your irrational fear of clowns isn't caused by some weird synapse misfiring in your brain. No, it's because a homicidal court jester actually attacked and killed your parents during your troubled childhood in sixteenth-century France. That totally explains it.[24]

1982, WASHINGTON, D.C.

William O'Neill, an electronics expert and alleged medium, teams up with a retired engineer named George Meek. And the two of them team up with a scientist named George Mueller. Only Mueller's

---

23. Wambach, Helen. *Reliving Past Lives: The Evidence Under Hypnosis* (New York: HarperCollins, 1978); Fiore, Edith. *You Have Been Here Before: A Psychologist Looks at Past Lives* (New York: Ballantine, 1978); Netherton, Morris. *Past Lives Therapy* (New York: Morrow, 1978).

24. In his book *Hidden Memories* (Prometheus, 1992), psychologist Robert Baker reveals that, based on an experiment he conducted, the people most likely to discover a whole mess of past lives during regression therapy are—wait for it—those who already believe in reincarnation. Awesome.

dead. He expired six years earlier, yet apparently is kind enough to assist them from beyond the grave. And despite the handicap of being one-third dead, the team is able to assemble an instrument they call Spiricom. What's a Spiricom? Why, it's a telephone to the afterlife!

At a Washington press conference, O'Neill announces that, with Mueller's help, he and Meek tuned the Spiricom to frequencies beyond the grave and thus were able to engage in more than thirty hours of voice-to-voice communication with the dead scientist. Then O'Neill throws down the gauntlet: He offers the schematics for building your own Spiricom to any researcher who also wants to converse with dead people. Bold move. Surprisingly, no one else can get it to work. Probably because they're not psychic like O'Neill. Or more likely, Mueller screens his Spiricom calls.

1985, UNITED STATES

Ruth Montgomery, an Indiana-born Christian psychic, remixes a little Hinduism and mysticism and New Agey goodness into several books about what she calls "walk-ins"—something that occurs when the original soul departs from a body (via a near-death experience, for instance, or profound trauma) and is replaced by another soul. And some of these squatter souls might be extraterrestrials! This is the horrible-sounding message of her book, *Aliens Among Us,* but it's not as bad as you think.[25] Because some of these alien walk-ins are kindly and wise, and they're here to help us get through these difficult times. Oh, and she predicts one of the U.S. presidents during the 1990s will be an extraterrestrial walk-in. So . . . George Bush the Elder or Bill Clinton? Right. It's totally Clinton.

---

25. Montgomery, Ruth S. *Aliens Among Us* (New York: Putnam, 1985).

1986, CALIFORNIA

According to a 1997 Gallup Poll, only 93 percent of Americans are certain that Elvis Presley is actually dead, despite the King having passed away of a drug overdose on August 16, 1977. Then again, Elvis' estate earned $52 million in 2008, according to the annual *Forbes* list of top-earning deceased celebrities. So maybe there's something to it.

Dr. Benito F. Reyes, the president of the World University of America, publishes a book called *Conscious Dying: Psychology of Death and Guidebook to Liberation,* in which he attempts to help people "pass through the process of death without losing consciousness."[26] He hopes his readers will achieve this worthy goal based on findings from his research on near-death and out-of-body experiences.[27] He also hopes lots of people will buy his book and read it to those on their deathbeds. This, he says, will give hope and peace to the nearly dead as they pass from one world into another. Hmm. Seeing how people are supposed to be fully conscious during this transition, one hopes it's a pleasant one. Maintaining consciousness as you tumble headlong into the black abyss of nonexistence can really screw up a person's liberation.

26. Reyes, Benito F. *Conscious Dying: Psychology of Death and Guidebook to Liberation* (Ojai, CA: World University of America, 1986).

27. He also founds the International Association for Conscious Dying in 1990. It has annual meetings and puts out a newsletter called Clear Light. You'll want to subscribe to it immediately at www.worldu.edu.

1997, CALIFORNIA

Failed opera singer Marshall Herff Applewhite spends a couple of decades building up a nice little cult since announcing in 1975 that he was a two-thousand-year-old alien. Over the years, he collects a bunch of followers who live with him in a house in Rancho Santa Fe, California, under the pleasant moniker "Heaven's Gate." The Gaters are mostly Web site–building computer nerds with shaved heads. They wear colorful jumpers. They wear matching tennis shoes. Oh, and the guys are all castrated.

Anyway, they live happy, sexless lives until amateur astronomer Chuck Shramek misidentifies a star as a "Saturn-like object" following the Hale-Bopp Comet in 1997. Shramek appears on the conspiracy-drenched Art Bell radio show, and before you know it, his "object" has been declared a UFO hiding in the comet's tail. This is exceedingly good news for the Heaven's Gate community, because it turns out Applewhite's late girlfriend, Bonnie Lu Nettles (who died of cancer in 1985), was a real live space alien. And she'd promised to stop by earth to pick them all up. She's on her way!

So the Heaven's Gate members plug in their video gear, record their goodbyes to family and friends, drop the VHS tapes in the mail, share a few spoonfuls of poisoned applesauce, and die in a mass suicide. Police receive a tip from a family member who gets spooked by the "I'm-leaving-on-a-spaceship" vibe of the goodbye video. And instead of a spaceship, the Gaters end up on the nightly news, complete with grim footage of each member stretched out dead on his or her cot, covered by a purple cloth.

2003, NEW YORK

Anthony DeStefano, a former electronics chain store president
and the executive director of the pro-life organization Priests for
Life, publishes *A Travel Guide to Heaven,* which goes on to become
a best seller.[28] It looks at heaven through a traditional Christian
lens, albeit with a dash of creativity to spice things up. For instance,
DeStefano is convinced heaven won't be the repetitive praising-
God-all-the-live-long-day paradise Christians often assume. Instead,
it'll be like a celestial cruise ship with countless entertainment and
excursion options—all of which will be led by celebrity experts.
The inhabitants of heaven will get to go fishing with Ernest Hem-
ingway, discuss literature with Jane Austen, or smoke cigars with
Winston Churchill. Bored after an eternity of those activities? Then
shake things up. Play catch with Joe DiMaggio. Ask Albert Einstein
to explain to you the theory of relativity. See if Mozart will teach
you to play the piano.

Of course, *A Travel Guide's* theory makes a couple of pretty big
assumptions. The first is that famous people like these actually make
heaven's roster in the first place. The second is that they'll be willing
to stick to DeStefano's plans. Sure, learning the piano from Mozart
sounds nice—to *you.* But the *Pocket Guide* doubts Mozart will be
that thrilled once he finds out his version of glory involves showing
a bunch of tin-eared dead folks how to play something more than
"Chopsticks."

One person's heaven? Might be a celebrity's hell.

---

28. DeStefano, Anthony. *A Travel Guide to Heaven* (New York: Bantam Dell, 2003).

2004, TEXAS

A Southern Baptist pastor named Don Piper publishes the best-selling *90 Minutes in Heaven,* a first-person account of his death, his quick trip to heaven, and his return.[29] Here's the story: Back in 1989, Piper entered a two-lane bridge on Texas Highway 19 over the Trinity River during a rain storm. He got hit head-on by an eighteen-wheeler. It slammed his Ford Escort against the railing and crushed half the vehicle beneath its wheels. When paramedics arrived, they saw Piper's mangled body, checked his pulse, failed to locate it, and pronounced him dead. But not so fast.

An hour-and-a-half later, another pastor arrived at the accident site. He felt God prompting him to pray for the dead guy, who'd been left in the vehicle, unattended to, while medical personnel focused on the surviving accident victims. So the pastor prayed. And sang some hymns, at which point Piper started singing with him.

The whole scenario is sorta Monty Python–esque, but it ends up being good news for Piper on at least two levels. First, he's most decidedly not dead, which is always a bonus. And second, his eventual book about the experience hits the big-time. *90 Minutes in Heaven* details the accident, Piper's painful recovery, and more than you want to know about what has happened to him since. Oh, and there's a brief description of heaven. But it's only, like, two short chapters. And it's nothing you haven't heard before. Brilliant light. Dazzling colors. A reception committee of friends and family. Indescribable joy. Ethereal music. Swooshing angels' wings. Sensory overload. Seriously, the book could have been titled

---

29. Piper, Don, with Cecil Murphey. *90 Minutes in Heaven: A True Story of Death and Life* (Grand Rapids, MI: Revell, 2004).

15 Pages About Heaven and Another 190 Pages of Filler You'll Find a Lot Less Interesting. But apparently someone finds it interesting, to the tune of more than 1.5 million copies sold by 2009.[30] Those royalty checks? Bliss.[31]

2006, CALIFORNIA

Not to be outdone by Piper, a real estate agent named Bill Wiese publishes his own book about spending a brief amount of time in another afterlifey place. Only he goes to hell. And while Wiese's book, *23 Minutes in Hell,* is also a best seller, it's not nearly as uplifting as Piper's.[32]

The story goes like this: In the early morning hours of November 23, 1998, Bill gets catapulted out of this dimension and plopped naked into hell. Without so much as a warning. (And it's not even a warm night.) He first lands in a terribly hot, dark cell, and unfortunately he's not alone. His cellmates? Two towering, reptilian demons. Who proceed to beat him up. And use their foot-long claws to tear his flesh into ribbons. And who smell really freaking bad. Eventually, Wiese escapes the cell only to be met by the deafening screams of millions of other condemned souls suffering eternal torment. He encounters a literal lake of fire, complete with showers of magma. Things are starting to look pretty bleak. But then Jesus shows up in a flash of light and informs Wiese that he—a lowly Realtor®—has

---

30. One might read between the lines of these sentences and get the sense that the *Pocket Guide* is jealous of Piper's success. And one would be right in making that assumption.

31. There's more about *90 Minutes in Heaven* in Chapter 7, on p. 183.

32. Wiese, Bill. *23 Minutes in Hell* ((Lake Mary, FL: Charisma House, 2006).

been chosen to deliver a message to mankind: that hell is real and they don't want to go there. Then Jesus removes Wiese from hell, shoots him up past the earth's surface all the way into space, and then plops him back down into his bed in California. Wiese wakes up screaming. And freaked out. And really thirsty.

Not wanting to disobey Jesus—who had gone to all that trouble to get his point across—Wiese spends the next few years sharing his gripping true-story-which-was-totally-not-a-bad-dream with anyone who'll listen. In 2006, he decides to share it with that portion of the world willing to fork over the $12.99 retail price. Hell of a deal.[33]

---

33. Read more about *23 Minutes in Hell* on p. 184 in Chapter 7.

CHAPTER 4

Geography of the Beyond
(Where You Might Go)

There are two big questions when it comes to the afterlife. The first is, obviously, *Who will feed my cats?* The second is *Where will I go?* And when that question is asked, it's rarely because we're thinking about particular cemeteries or funeral homes or mortuaries. No, we have the bigger picture in mind. And it's not enough to assume we'll encounter a conscious existence after death. We want to know what that existence will be like. Will it be blissful, bright, and beautiful? Will it be hot and dusty? Will we be set on fire by demons?

When questioned about eternal destinations, most people are optimistic. According to a 2004 Gallup Poll, 81 percent of Americans believe in heaven, and 77 percent of those think they have a good chance of ending up there. On the subject of hell, 70 percent believe it exists. But hardly anyone thinks they've got reservations for the place.

The *Pocket Guide* was unable to find any polls revealing how many people believe they're headed to Niflheim.

Nevertheless, the Viking underworld is a potential destination in the afterlife. So is Swarga. And Diyu. And Naraka. And Tlalocan. Heaven and hell may get all the press (and each gets its own chapter in a few pages), but if human history is any indication, those two biggies are not the only options when it comes to the afterlife. Besides, if you die and pass into another realm where you find yourself wearing feathers, or being ground into powder, or being pursued by a demon with hippo legs, then you're gonna want to know where you've ended up.

Here, then, is a not-quite-comprehensive but wide-ranging list of the rest stops on the eternal highway. Some of them are lovely. A few are sketchy. And at least one involves a corpse-sucking dragon, so plan accordingly.

Celestial Kingdom

What it is: The highest of the three Mormon heavenly kingdoms or "degrees of glory" where the righteous will spend eternity after the final resurrection. Unlike the *Telestial* and *Terrestrial Kingdoms*, the Celestial Kingdom is for those Mormons who follow all the rules, and then some. God and Jesus live in the Celestial Kingdom, so it's a place of profound glory and wonderment. This is where you want to end up. This is also why Mormons are always trying to get you to join their ranks. It's for your own good.

Where it is: Probably on earth, after the planet has been refurbished into something more glorious in the age to come.

How to get there: Two ways. First, if you die before the age of eight, you automatically qualify for entrance. Which is kinda sad, but preferable in an eternal sense. Second, you must die having met certain Mormon-ish qualifications. These include adherence to all the teachings of the faith and maintaining that faith all the way to the end.

Most important, you have to have been sealed in celestial marriage in an elaborate ritual in a sanctioned Mormon temple. According to the Mormon faith, celestial marriage is a marriage that lasts not just until you die but long long *long* after that, throughout eternity. It's either one of the best or most frightening ideas in all of Mormonism, depending on your perspective. Or your spouse.

HELPFUL TIPS

The only way women make it into the Celestial Kingdom is on their husband's coattails—the man must "resurrect" his wife and invite her in. So make sure you get married, and stay married . . . and make sure your husband behaves. If he doesn't make heaven? Neither do you.

What it's like: The Celestial Kingdom is divided into three levels. The highest level is the goal of all Mormons, because it involves becoming some sort of god-like being yourself and getting your own planet to run (and populate!) with the help of your forever wife and your family. No, really. The other levels are nice and everything, but it's hard to compete with everlasting family time and the planet-owning deity-ness. As for the other two Celestial levels, the Mormon scriptures don't say much about them. But you can bet they're super-glorious.

Surprise: When good Mormons get to their version of heaven, they'll be known by a new name. This name was given to them at the time of their celestial wedding, and they must never pronounce it again on earth. Unfortunately, it's not a cool rule-your-own-planet name like Voltar or Megatron or Kevin. It's usually a dull biblical one. Adam is popular, as is Peter. The biblical name Zeeb is less popular.[1]

Celestial Paradise of the Rising and/or Setting Sun

What it is: The post-death destination for the most virtuous and heroic Aztec warriors and their women.

Where it is: In, on, or around the sun.

How to get there: If you're male, you must be a warrior who dies in battle, a victim of human sacrifice to the gods, or a tradesman who dies while out on a journey. You'll be cremated and sent to the eastern half of the sky where the sun rises.

If you're female, you must die in childbirth, get cremated, then go toward the western half of the sky where the sun sets. Sorry, kids. There will be no intersexual mingling in the afterlife.

What it's like: Hot and bright. But in a good way. Every morning, before sunrise, the guys dress up in their warrior outfits

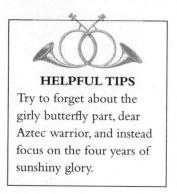

HELPFUL TIPS

Try to forget about the girly butterfly part, dear Aztec warrior, and instead focus on the four years of sunshiny glory.

---

1. Judges 7:25.

and accompany the sun from first light until midday. Then they hand it off to the women, who escort the sun down to the western horizon.

Surprise: After four years of this sun–accompaniment, you and all your dead warrior friends turn into butterflies and birds and return to earth to drink nectar from flowers.

Chinvat Bridge

What it is: The place of final judgment in Zoroastrianism. As expected, it's a bridge. Souls must cross it in order to get to Paradise.

Where it is: One side supposedly begins at the top of "Mount Alborz" in northern Iran, which sounds pretty simple until you learn that "Alborz" is the name of the entire mountain range stretching from Armenia to the Caspian Sea.[2] The other side of the bridge? It's attached to Paradise. Good luck finding it, too.

How to get there: Some three days after death, your soul begins a journey to the bridge. Once your soul arrives—and if you're righteous—you will be given passage over the bridge and into

Based on the current world population, approximately 250,000 people die every day. That's almost 11,000 people an hour. Or 180 every minute. Or 3 dead people every second. Cheers!

---

2. Random Information Alert: You will probably be surprised to find out that some of the best ski resorts in the world are located in this range. The *Pocket Guide SO* wants a "Ski Iran" bumper sticker.

Paradise. But if you're wicked, your soul will plummet off the bridge and into the torments of hell. If you are exactly as wicked as you are righteous—if your earthly sins and good deeds somehow balance each other out perfectly, and however you achieved that, *well done*—then you go to a place called Hamistagan ("region of the mixed"), where you wait around for the apocalypse.

HELPFUL TIPS

Stock up on those good deeds while you can. Or better yet, convert to a non-Zoroastrian religion.

What it's like: According to some texts, you're met on the bridge by a personification of your deeds. So if you performed good works in life, you encounter a beautiful maiden who smiles at you, takes your hand, and shows you the way to Paradise. If you were a sinful turdbag, you encounter a hideous, wretched old woman. She pokes you in the eye, kicks you in the nuts, and then tosses you over the side of the bridge and into hell.

Surprise: You wouldn't think the shriveled hag could take you, but she's freakishly strong.

Diyu

What it is: The hellish abode in ancient Chinese mythology where souls end up between reincarnated lives. According to most accounts, Diyu has ten different underground courts or levels, with the tenth court itself divided into eighteen chambers. Each chamber corresponds to a certain sin (though it's disputed as to whether all these chambers and levels are parts of the same hell or actual separate hells). The purpose of these pits of punishment is to get souls all cleaned up for their next reincarnation.

Where it is: Subterranean.

How to get there: Your soul automatically zaps into it, after death.

What it's like: Your time in Diyu is temporary, but while you're actually there it is nothing less than pretty freaking horrible. Punishments include being

HELPFUL TIPS

Go to p. 191 and read for yourself a complete list of the eighteen chambers of Diyu's Tenth Court. At least that way you'll know what kind of ghastly treatment to expect.

encased in ice, being sawed in half, being ground into powder, and being forced to climb a mountain of knives. Oh yes. A mountain of knives.

Surprise: Mountain. Of. Knives.

Duat

What it is: The ancient Egyptian underworld. Most of the action in Duat takes place at the Judgment Hall of Osiris, also known as the Hall of the Two Truths.

Where it is: A parallel dimension, accessible only by the soul. And the gods.

How to get there: You die, but you don't end up there immediately. First, your soul must pass through a bunch of tricky tests, helpfully described in detail in the Egyptian *Book of the Dead*, which your relatives should have left for you in your tomb. After passing through the underworld, you end up before Osiris, the judge of the dead. He's accompanied by several dozen other gods, including Maat, the feathery headdress-wearing goddess who personifies truth, justice, and the ancient Egyptian way.

What it's like: So you recite the Negative Confession[3] there in front of Osiris and Maat and everybody. Then some mystical scales are wheeled out. Osiris places your heart in one scale. Maat places a feather in another scale. Next comes an eternally significant moment of dread as you wait to see which item—heart or feather—weighs the most. If your heart weighs less than or the same as the feather, that's good news: You get to pass through to Aaru, the Field of Reeds. But if your heart weighs more than Maat's magic feather, that's bad news, because clearly you are sinful and your heart is encumbered with bad mojo . . .

HELPFUL TIPS

Switching to a heart-healthy diet? Not a bad idea.

Surprise: . . . at which point your heart and soul will immediately be devoured by the horrifying demon goddess Ammut, also known as the "eater of the dead." Ammut looks pretty much like you'd expect an eater of the dead to look. She has the head of a crocodile, the chest and front legs of a lion, and the stout back legs of a hippo. These mashed-up body parts represented the three creatures the ancient Egyptians feared most.[4]

---

3. A litany of the sins you have not committed, thought to be a pretty effective way to make sure Osiris, Maat, and other deities recognized your worthiness of the Field of Reeds. See pp. 28–29 in Chapter 1.

4. To contemporary Americans, Ammut would probably have the torso of a grizzly bear, the tail of a rattlesnake, and the head of Osama bin Laden.

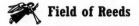 **Field of Reeds**

What it is: The ancient Egyptian paradise, also known as Aaru. Apparently, it looks a lot like the Nile Delta, only more sparkly.

Where it is: In the east, where the sun rises.

How to get there: First, you have to pass the ridiculously stressful feather test of Maat in the Judgment Hall of Osiris, which the *Pocket Guide* just described. Then you pass through a series of gates—at least fifteen of them—all guarded by demons with long knives. Once you've put the demons in your rearview mirror, it's all happy bliss.

What it's like: The Field of Reeds is home to lovely palaces, fertile fishing grounds, productive hunting, and is the dwelling place of Osiris and all the other gods. Also, it's entirely free of anything resembling a hippo–legged crocodile/lion demon intent on devouring your soul. That's always good.

Surprise: It may be paradise, but you have to *work* in Aaru. Like back-breaking agricultural work. Fields must be tilled, water must be transferred, and crops must be tended. Even worse? This work takes place for *eternity*. Oh my. Someone tell the ancient Egyptians they designed their paradise all wrong.

HELPFUL TIPS

Make sure your relatives follow the ancient Egyptian custom of filling your tomb with *ushabti,* wee little statues who will become your magical servants in the afterlife. That's right—these cute manmade dopple-gangers come to life and do the heavy labor on your behalf. Then you can just lounge around all the live-long day, sunbathing in the reeds and swimming in the Nile and playing shuffle-board with Osiris.

Hades

What it is: The vast, multichambered underworld of Greek mythology, featuring several different subdivisions for its residents.

HELPFUL TIPS

Steer clear of Cerberus, the three-headed, snake-tailed dog who guards the opposite side of the River Styx. He makes sure no dead people try to sneak back into the land of the living. Also? Don't let one of those three heads lick you. Cerberus has poisonous slobber.

One of these neighborhoods, the Elysian Fields, is an exclusive enclave reserved for the heroic and virtuous.[5] A good place to go. Bad people end up in Tartarus, the gloomy pit of torment reserved for sinners.[6] Ordinary folks who aren't quite heroic enough for the Elysian Fields or naughty enough for Tartarus end up milling around in the Fields of Asphodel. Which sounds nice and everything, but it's mostly covered with grayish plants dotted with ghostly white flowers. It's dull and purposeless and creepy, and the parties there are totally lame compared with the stuff going down in the Elysian Fields.

Where it is: Underground. Probably beneath Greece.

---

5. It should be noted that some Greek myths place the Elysian Fields in Hades, but others locate them on islands resting on the far western edge of the earth near a river called Oceanus. These islands are sometimes called the Isles of the Blessed, or the Fortunate Isles, or Fiji.

6. Occasionally, Tartarus will be combined in mythology with a place called Erebus. Sometimes there's no distinction between the two. Other times Erebus refers to the place the dead go immediately upon dying. It's like the foyer to hell.

How to get there: After death, Hermes (the Greek god of travelers and boundaries, among other things) guides your soul to the edge of the mystically powerful River Styx. A demonic winged ferryman named Charon[7] then takes you across the river, for a small fee. You should be prepared for this, because your relatives are supposed to have put gold coins over your eyes when they buried you. If they forgot or refused to follow the custom, then you're out of luck: your soul has to wander the banks of the Styx for the next hundred years. It sucks being poor *and* dead.

What it's like: According to most reports, life in Hades—even the non-torturous parts—is but a shadow of the life you used to live.

Surprise: Hades is crisscrossed by rivers. Not just the Styx but the Lethe (which makes you forget your past life when you drink from it), the Acheron (the "river of woe" that forms the border to Tartarus), the Cocytus (the "river of wailing," which may or may not be frozen), and the flaming Phlegython (which empties into Tartarus).[8] Also watch for the famous trees of Hades, including the white cypresses near the palace of Hades and Persephone (the king and queen of the underworld), the black poplars at the gates of Tartarus, the beautiful orchards of the Elysian Fields, and the occasional weeping willow (natch).

 ## Irkalla

What it is: The gloomy netherworld of Mesopotamian/Sumerian mythology, ruled first by the goddess Ereshkigal, the

---

7. Sometimes known as Phlegyas, which isn't nearly as cool of a name. Also not as cool? Sometimes Charon is just a grumpy old man, not a winged demon.

8. In Dante's *Inferno,* the Phlegython is a boiling river of blood that consumes the souls of murderers.

naked black-skinned queen of darkness, until she was overthrown by Nergal. Nergal had a lion head, was the god of pestilence and death, and even gets a shout-out in the Bible.[9]

Where it is: Underground.

How to get there: By passing through seven gates, each of which requires you to leave a toll. The preferred payment? Your clothes—including loin-cloths and girdles—along with necklaces, bracelets, and other blingy embellishments. You won't need these anymore because your existence in Irkalla will be one of total darkness. And because you'll be decomposing anyway. And, oh, because you'll be dressed in feathers. Feathers clash with just about everything.

What it's like: Again, it's dark. It's gloomy. It's decompose-y. You'll spend your time dining on dust and drinking clay. And probably getting all itchy due to those feathers, and what's up with them anyway?

Surprise: You'll probably run into the evil demon Namtar at

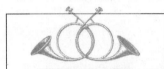

HELPFUL TIPS

Don't gawk at Namtar's hand- and footlessness. In fact, just stay away from him altogether. This is a good general rule when it comes to plague demons, especially those who are not likely to cover up a sneeze or hacking cough on account of them having no hands. Talk about impolite.

---

9. 2 Kings 17:29–30 NIV: "Nevertheless, each national group made its own gods in the several towns where they settled, and set them up in the shrines the people of Samaria had made at the high places. The men from Babylon made Succoth Benoth, the men from Cuthah made Nergal . . ."

some point, because he's Ereshkigal's chief minister, messenger, and feather-wrangler. He's also considered a bringer of disease and pestilence. He has no hands or feet.

Jahannam

What it is: The Islamic version of hell. The name *Jahannam* sounds a lot like *Gehenna,* the Greek word translated "hell" in the Christian New Testament. Jahannam has seven layers. Kind of like the dip, but dramatically less delicious.

Where it is: On the underside of the world.

HELPFUL TIPS

Be patient. The Qu'ran seems to teach that the fiery punishments of Jahannam aren't necessarily eternal but could eventually stop once you've been purified and/ or forgiven. Wear cool, heat-wicking clothing, try to dine on as few demon fruits as possible, and wait it out.

How to get there: Refuse to believe in Allah, or be an unfaithful Muslim. Either of those sends you there after the day of resurrection.

What it's like: It's a place of boiling water and cinders and ashes and skin-meltingly literal fire. And according to the Qu'ran, this fire burns seventy times hotter than earthly fire, thanks to a nontraditional fuel source: rocks. And also people.

Surprise: Don't miss Zaqqum, the horrible-smelling tree in Jahannam, because it's not just any regular old supernatural tree. It's a hell-tree! This means it blossoms not with flowers but with the heads of demons.[10] And if you eat its fruit? The stuff turns to white-hot liquid metal in your belly and shreds your intestines. Pretty darn creative as far as punishments go. Good job, Islam.

 Jannah

What it is: The Islamic equivalent of Heaven. *Jannah* is Arabic for "garden." It contains at least eight levels, with the highest ones devoted to martyrs, prophets, and the super-pious.

---

10. There is some confusion as to whether the blossoms are literally the heads of demons or if they are only shaped like demon heads. Some traditions maintain it's only the fruit that's demon-head-shaped, not the blossoms. During such uncertainty, the *Pocket Guide* always chooses to err on the side of actual demon heads, as a rule. So it's the first option.

Where it is: Unknown. Probably another dimension.

How to get there: Believe in Allah and the prophets, and perform acts of righteousness during your life on earth. If Allah wills, you'll go to Jannah after the Day of Judgment.

What it's like: It's pretty nice. Everything that brought a person pleasure on earth will exist in abundance in paradise. All wishes will be fulfilled, all sorrow and pain will disappear, and everyone will be thirty-three years old. (Which everyone knows is the best age ever.) In Jannah, you'll enjoy frequent banquets and have access to scrumptious fruits and rivers of milk, honey, and non-intoxicating wine. You'll wear the finest clothes—including silver bracelets and silk robes—while dwelling in swanky palaces complete with comfy thrones and rich carpets and cushiony cushions.

Surprise: The foods you eat in Jannah won't produce waste, only sweet-smelling sweat. This will make you more attractive to

In Islam, the serious post-death action kicks off at Judgment Day, but don't discount what happens once they close the casket on your funeral. As soon as you die, you get interrogated by Munkar and Nakir, two faith-testing angels who get all up in your business while you're still trying to figure out if you're really dead or just dreaming. They pepper you with questions like "Who is your Lord?" (answer: Allah), "Who is your prophet?" (Muhammad), and "What is your religion?" (Islam). Answer properly and your time in the grave won't seem so long. And while you're waiting it out, you'll enjoy a few appetizing peeks at the glory that awaits you. Like a heavenly sampler plate. Answer wrongly, though? That would be unfortunate. Munkar and Nakir scold you mercilessly until Judgment comes. And you know what they say on the streets of Mecca: Ain't nothin' worse than the mockery of Islamic prosecuting angels.

the countless voluptuous *houri*[11] available to you in Paradise, with whom you'll be allowed to have everlasting nookie. And you'll be able to handle it, because you'll be given the nookie-having strength of a hundred men.[12]

Limbo

What it is: A theoretical state in Catholic theology that's not quite heaven and not quite hell. The idea developed early in Christianity when the early Church couldn't figure out what to do with two kinds of dead people: unbaptized babies (who were born into original sin but were way too young to be, like, evil or anything) and the righteous men and women of the faith (like Abraham, Moses, and David) who died before Jesus showed up to save them—salvation through Christ being a prerequisite for heaven.

Where it is: On the borderlands between heaven and hell. In fact, the name comes from the Latin word *limbus,* which means both "border" and "popular luau game."

How to get there: Die as a baby before your Catholic family gets the chance to baptize you. Or, die as a biblical Patriarch.[13]

What it's like: It's either a permanent or temporary state, depending on who you are. Because heaven was believed to only be available through the shed blood of Jesus, the righteous "heroes"

---

11. You should have read about *houri* on p. 24 in Chapter 1. If you didn't, then quit skipping around already.

12. If you find yourself asking what kinds of physical benefits are available to female Muslims in paradise, you are not alone. Unfortunately, in the Qu'ran, most of the delights seem to be male-centric.

13. Granted, this may be a difficult task for readers of this book.

of the faith had to hang out here until Jesus was born, crucified, and resurrected. By the time this finally went down, Abraham had gotten seriously grouchy. This holding facility was commonly known as the "Limbo of the Fathers."

For babies, though, Limbo is permanent. No one wanted to see a baby burn in everlasting fire.

HELPFUL TIPS

Sure, it's not hell, but an abode of the dead filled wall-to-wall with crying pooping screaming babies? No picnic. Avoid if possible.

But everyone also agreed that unbaptized sinners, especially those born into the sinful human race but who probably never performed *actual* sins, are technically excluded from salvation. So they've gotta go somewhere. Why not send them to a place that's not especially heavenly but also not excruciatingly hot? So pretty much Limbo used to be filled with dead guys from the Old Testament. Now it's filled with a bunch of babies.

Surprise: Limbo gained a lot of traction among medieval Christians, but most Catholics don't put much stock in it anymore.[14] The general teaching of the Roman Catholic Church today is that the sacrament of baptism is required for salvation, but God doesn't have to follow his own rules. Which means unbaptized infants (and their grieving families) are dependent on the mercy of God. And seriously, what kind of God would send a baby to hell?

---

14. Belief in Limbo is an optional doctrine for Catholics. It's one of several theological options they can choose from when it comes to the classic *what-happens-to-babies?* question

Mictlan

What it is: The dark realm in Aztec mythology where souls go after they die. It's ruled by Mictlantecuhtli, the bloody, skeletal god of death who wears a necklace of human eyeballs. He's joined by his queen/assistant Mictecacihuatl, also known as the Lady of the Dead. Her choice of neckware is unknown.[15]

Where it is: In the lowest, northernmost section of the Aztec underworld.

How to get there: First, die a "normal" death, according to the Aztecs. This means expiring due to old age or illness. But that's just the first step, because there's a long journey ahead of you. First, your corpse is bundled up in cloth and paper and cremated, along with a dog companion. Then you and Fido-cihuatl spend the next four years winding your way through nine different subterranean layers. You'll cross mountains, defend yourself against wild animals, and fight howling winds. Then you get there and the doors lock behind you. Also? There are no exits. Welcome to Mictlan! Enjoy your eternity!

HELPFUL TIPS

Mictlantecuhtli and Mictecacihuatl supposedly live in a house in the middle of Mictlan.[16] It's worth a trip there, because pretty much it's the only thing to see.

---

15. Early Aztec "Festivals of the Dead" in honor of Mictecacihuatl eventually morphed into today's traditional "Day of the Dead" in Mexico. (That's *El Día de los Muertos* for Spanish readers of the *Pocket Guide*.)
16. Hell for the *Pocket Guide* is being forced to type Mictlantecuhtli and Mictecacihuatl over and over

What it's like: The inside of a fireplace. It's dark, gloomy, and filled with soot and ash. But at least there's no fire.

Surprise: The Aztecs occasionally worshiped Mictlantecuhtli by eating human flesh in their temple. And you thought your church's potluck suppers were distasteful.

Naraka

What it is: The Hindu underworld, where naughty souls are tormented and/or punished for the sins they've committed in their previous life. It's ruled by Yama, the Hindu demigod of death and justice.

Where it is: At the bottom of the universe, near the mythical Garbhodaka Ocean.

How to get there: First, you die. No surprise there. But what *is* surprising is *how* you die. At the precise second of death, creepy little red-haired and black-faced servants of Yama—called *yamadutas*—arrive on the scene, metaphysically speaking. They tangle a bunch of chains and ropes around you and start yanking your soul out of your body and into the dark Beyond. This is apparently so unimaginably frightening that the Stephen King-ness of it actually kills you. That's right: you get scared to death. You don't die from whatever else (sickness, oncoming train) was about to deal the death blow. Nope, you die because of the little nightmare munchkins.

Anyway, once they've scared the living moksha out of you, they pack up your soul and deliver it to Naraka, where Yama will judge it. This is a long journey, and your soul is conscious of it the whole time. Along the way you endure numerous trials, including bites

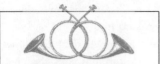

HELPFUL TIPS
If you're having trouble figuring out which fearsome deity is Yama, look for the green-skinned, red-eyed demigod perched on the back of a water buffalo. He has a rod in one hand and a noose in the other. The noose? Probably one of the ropes used to extract the soul from your corpse.

from Yama's four-eyed devil dogs. When you finally reach Yama, it's a relief.[17]

What it's like: . . . but the relief doesn't last long. Depending on how bad you were, Yama assigns you a punishment in one of the hellish regions of Naraka. This punishment may involve, for instance, your transformation into a worm that's eating the tail of another worm who is, in turn, eating *your* tail. Or it could involve you boiling in oil. Once you've been suitably punished, your fresh, shiny soul gets shipped back to earth and into some low species of life—a parasitic intestinal tapeworm, perhaps—that suits your previous behavior.

Surprise: The legendary Hindu figure Vamanadeva once kicked a powerful demon named Ravana 80,000 miles using only his big toe.[18]

---

17. These details courtesy of the Bhagavata Purana, an ancient, frightening, and perilously entertaining Hindu text. See www.vedabase.net/sb.

18. This is a tale out of Hindu mythology, but honestly it has nothing to do with Naraka. The *Pocket Guide* just liked it and wanted to insert that sentence into this book. Done.

Niflheim

What it is: The Viking "abode of mist," or underworld. It's presided over by Hel, the sinister Norse giantess who is half-black and half-white, like an Oreo. If an Oreo wasn't a delicious cookie but instead was a dreadful goddess of death.[19]

Where it is: It's hidden under the sacred ash tree Yggdrasil, also known as the "tree of the world" located in the center of the universe. Yggdrasil has three roots. Niflheim is underneath the third root.

How to get there: Just die . . . as long as your death is ordinary and not heroic by any means. You could die of sickness, if you want. Or of old age. Or you could die of a heart attack while eating a bacon double-cheeseburger. Any of these is acceptable, as long as you don't die courageously, or in battle, or in any spectacular manner. Because

HELPFUL TIPS

Unless a corpse-sucking dragon sounds appealing, all Vikings should start making plans now to die in an act of noble gallantry.

an awesome, valiant death earns you a seat in the anti-Niflheim, otherwise known as Valhalla.

What it's like: Boring. Cold. Covered with ice.

Surprise: Niflheim is guarded by the monstrous hellhound Garm. And in the same neighborhood as Niflheim is a place called

---

19. Most etymologists think the English word *hell* is derived from her name. Sounds about right.

Nastrond ("the shore of corpses"), where the dragon Nidhogg chews on the roots of Yggdrasil and "sucks the corpses of the dead."[20] Crikey.

 Purgatory

What it is: The realm in the Christian Catholic tradition where the souls of the dead are purified, via punishment, in order to clean them up for heaven. People who die in mortal sin go to hell. People who die in a state of grace go to heaven. People who aren't mortal sinners but aren't sinless enough for heaven go to Purgatory. It's related to the idea of Limbo, but it's temporary. And there aren't so many babies.

Where it is: Unknown. In the *Divine Comedy,* Dante claimed Purgatory was a mountain in the southern hemisphere. But in a Wednesday-morning General Audience in 1999, Pope John Paul II proclaimed that Purgatory wasn't a physical place but a condition of existence.[21] Take that, Dante.

> **HELPFUL TIPS**
>
> If you see a ghost, ask him or her about Purgatory. Because many religious folk believe they are souls still in the process of being cleansed. If you see a fat ghost running to and fro, you will know this is true.

---

20. This according to Benjamin Thorpe's 1866 translation of The *Edda of Sæmund the Learned (*available online at http://www.northvegr.org/lore/poetic2/000.php).

21. August 4, 1999 (transcript available at www.vatican.va).

How to get there: Die having committed only *venial sins*—forgivable moral failures that are sorta frowned upon but don't really set you up as an enemy of God—but having failed to attain forgiveness for them through the sacraments of the Church.

What it's like: Not so great. Purgatory is usually associated with cleansing, but it's not a refreshing loofah-and-shower-gel cleansing. It's fire. Fire hotter than the hottest flame you've ever experienced on earth. The pain is more painful than any pain you've ever had. But it's a happy kind of pain, because the result of it is glorious.

Despite having been declared full of crap by the pope, Dante's depictions of Purgatory are worth reading. In his version, each of the seven deadly sins has a specific and creative punishment. The slothful, for instance, have to run and run and run all over the place while weeping uncontrollably. It's like a really loooong, uncomfortable class at the gym.[22]

Surprise: The doctrine of Purgatory played a major role in the Protestant Reformation. In the Middle Ages, the Church began selling indulgences, which allowed the bearers to bypass some of the punishments of Purgatory earlier than required. (*Attention, all ye slothful: Redeem one indulgence and we'll knock three laps off your punishment!*) Due to a widespread abuse of this doctrine, the Martin Luther–led Protestant Reformers got all huffy and threw out this religious baby and the bathwater associated with it, from certain books of the Bible (Purgatory-supportive Apocrypha) to veneration of the Virgin Mary, Queen of Purgatory.

---

22. For more on the sadistic torments of Dante's purgatory and hell, see pp. 185–186 and pp. 188–189 in the last chapter.

"He that eateth well drinketh well,
he that drinketh well sleepeth well,
he that sleepeth well sinneth not,
he that sinneth not goeth straight through Purgatory to Paradise."

WILLIAM LITHGOW (1582–1645), SCOTTISH TRAVELER AND POET

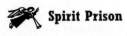 **Spirit Prison**

HELPFUL TIPS

If you find yourself in Spirit Prison, pay attention. If you get baptized by proxy back on earth, you'll definitely want to know about it so you can take advantage of that ticket out.

What it is: The Mormon hell, also known as "outer darkness."[23] Very few people are wicked enough to end up there forever—most go to one of the three degrees of glory known as the *Celestial, Terrestrial,* and *Telestial Kingdoms*—but those who do go to Spirit Prison are known as "sons of perdition." Which would be an excellent name for a bluegrass band (*Live Tonight from Provo: Donny Osmond & the Sons of Perdition!*).

---

23. From Matthew 8:12: "But the subjects of the kingdom will be thrown outside, into the darkness, where there will be weeping and gnashing of teeth" (KJV). See also Matthew 22:13 and 25:30.

Where it is: An alternate dimension. Nowhere near Provo.

How to get there: Die having rejected Jesus Christ and the teachings of the Church of Jesus Christ of Latter-Day Saints. You'll go to Spirit Prison immediately to atone for your sins while you await the final resurrection.

What it's like: The three biblical descriptions of the "outer darkness" attach it to the phrase "weeping and gnashing of teeth," so it's definitely a place of torment. And destructive dental habits. In Mormon theology, Spirit Prison is referenced in two different ways. The first is as a temporary holding place for sinners. Yes, *temporary,* because not all is lost. Residents still have a chance, in between

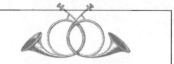

HELPFUL TIPS

Whatever you do, don't commit the "unpardonable sin" during your stay in Spirit Prison. That's the only thing that keeps you locked up in outer darkness and prevents you from reaching heaven. And while that's good advice and everything, there's some confusion over what an unpardonable sin would actually entail. Some think it's murder. Others think it's a second round of adultery after you've already played your first "it was just a stupid mistake and won't happen again" card. Most Mormons think the unpardonable sin involves having your eyes opened to the truth of salvation—that is, getting the chance, even in hell, to choose faith—but denying it anyway. Cold. That's blasphemy against the Holy Ghost, and it earns you eternity in fire and brimstone.

teeth-gnashings, to believe and repent of their sins and even to be baptized by proxy, thanks to a thoughtful still-living relative.[24]

The second belief about Spirit Prison is that it's an eternal holding cell for the sons of perdition (Donny Osmond excluded)—those who reject belief on earth *and* in hell. It's also where the devil and his minions end up, roasting eternally in a lake of fire and brimstone.

Surprise: Along with Satan, the list of everlasting residents of Spirit Prison includes famed first murderer Cain, the son of Adam who brained his brother Abel in Genesis 4.

Swarga

What it is: The Hindu version of heaven, where your soul hangs out in blissful relaxation before the next round of reincarnating drops. Swarga is ruled by Indra, the god of thunder and lightning. A bunch of other gods live there, too.

Where it is: At the top of Mt. Meru, the sacred mountain at the center of the universe. Mt. Meru is supposedly 279,000 miles high. In comparison, Mt. Everest is 5.5 miles high. So Meru is pretty hard to miss.

How to get there: Die with good karma.

What it's like: It's paradise. Your soul feasts on the fruits of your good deeds from your previous life. Then, after a nice rest, you get sent back to earth. And sure, you're departing the land of milk and honey and fruity karmic goodness, but back on earth your soul will

---

24. This is known as "baptism for the dead" and it has to be performed in certain, specially dedicated Mormon temples. It's even mentioned in the Bible, in 1 Corinthians 15:29. The presence of this verse often surprises Christians, who tend to think the whole concept is crazy talk.

get downloaded into a higher species of life. Like a bald eagle. Or a cheetah. Or Tiger Woods.

Telestial Kingdom

What it is: The lowest of the three levels of Mormon heaven, below the highest *Celestial Kingdom* and the next-highest *Terrestrial Kingdom*. The Telestial Kingdom is a highly populated one. It's reserved for pretty much everyone who's ever lived, because it's where sinful people eventually end up after atoning for their unrighteousness in *Spirit Prison*.

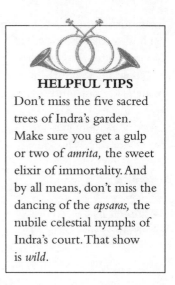

HELPFUL TIPS

Don't miss the five sacred trees of Indra's garden. Make sure you get a gulp or two of *amrita,* the sweet elixir of immortality. And by all means, don't miss the dancing of the *apsaras,* the nubile celestial nymphs of Indra's court. That show is *wild*.

Where it is: Another dimension

How to get there: Get born. Give in to your carnal desires. Embrace the vain philosophies of this world rather than following Jesus and his prophet Joseph Smith and the teachings of the Book of Mormon. Do other bad stuff. Die. Atone for that bad stuff for a thousand years in the hellish hotness of Spirit Prison. Be among the last to get resurrected at the End Times. Rejoice. Then live forever in the Telestial Kingdom.

What it's like: Well, it's a type of heaven, and it's more glorious than anything you've ever known, but it's less glorious than the other two heavens. The presence of God and Jesus are noticeably absent, but the presence of the third member of the Trinity—the Holy Spirit—is evident. Also evident? That you're surrounded

123

by murderers, thieves, adulterers, blasphemers, and reality show applicants. Probably not what you figured heaven would be like. But still better than the alternative.

Surprise: So pretty much everyone—even the really awful members of humanity—achieves immortality and ends up in some level of heaven. For all the strictness about tobacco and alcohol and Osmond fandom, the Mormons are pretty easygoing when it comes to the Afterlife. Who knew?

Terrestrial Kingdom

What it is: The second of the three levels of Mormon heaven, a notch above the *Telestial Kingdom* and below the glorious *Celestial Kingdom*. The Terrestrial Kingdom is for nice people of other religions (or no religion at all) who reject the Mormon faith but live a virtuous life anyhow. It's also for those who convert to Mormonism after death.

Where it is: Another dimension.

How to get there: See above. You die after having lived a decent life, but you were blinded by a false religion and probably concluded the whole ruling-your-own-planet thing was a load of crap (or "a load of hogwash," depending on what your religion thought about strong language). Or you were extra bad and went to hell, but a quick-thinking Mormon relative back on earth stepped up and got you baptized by proxy. Either of these things gets you into the Terrestrial Kingdom. But first you have to pay for your sins by doing time in *Spirit Prison*.

What it's like: Interestingly, the Terrestrial level of the kingdom is often compared to the moon. It gives off more light than the stars (Telestial Kingdom) but only *reflects* the light of the sun (Celestial

Kingdom).You get to enjoy the full presence of Jesus but not the full glory of God. Also, you don't get your own planet, which blows.

Surprise: The Terrestrial Kingdom will be inhabited by Christians who didn't accept the teachings of the Latter-Day Saints. So it's probably pretty close to regular heaven, only everyone's a little disappointed.

 Tlalocan

What it is: The Aztec paradise, ruled by Tlaloc, the god of rain, water, lightning, and fertility. He's usually depicted with fangs and googly eyes. Like an insane Muppet werewolf with a feathery crown. He's married to Chalchiuhtlicue, the Aztec goddess of lakes, streams, childbirth, and unpronounceable names.

Where it is: On level four of the thirteen-level upper paradise of Aztec mythology.

How to get there: Die in a particular manner. Spots in Tlalocan may be reserved for those who die of lightning strike, drowning, or water-related diseases

HELPFUL TIPS

Somewhere within the multiple levels of paradise—and possibly within Tlalocan—there is a tree of breasts. It has breast-shaped fruit, and all the not-yet-weaned children tend to hang out here. Literally. They hang from it, latched onto the fruit. This is not something you see every day, especially in heaven, so it's worth some exploration.[25]

---

25. If you don't find it in Tlalocan, the tree of breasts may also be located on the eleventh level of paradise.

like edema. Yes, it was *that* specific. Then you must be buried—not cremated—usually in a seated position with a wooden stick, which immediately becomes all leafy and flowery when you get to Tlalocan. You may also end up in Tlalocan if you die in infancy, before you've been weaned.

What it's like: It's a beautiful tropical garden with edible plants, abundant sunshine, spring-like temperatures, and an absence of sorrow.

Surprise: You ended up here, instead of the dreary *Mictlan,* because you died of edema instead of some other random illness. Praise Tlaloc for swelling caused by an excess of interstitial fluid.

Valhalla

What it is: The Viking heaven, also known as the "hall of the slain," which belongs to Norse über-god Odin. It's available to the spirits of those who died gloriously on the battlefield, and also to their women.

Where it is: In a region of Asgard called Gladsheim. Asgard is the realm of the gods, and it's near one of the roots of Yggdrasil, the humongous sacred ash tree in the center of the universe.

How to get there: Are you a mighty warrior? Then you can get to Valhalla by dying in battle, at which point you will be escorted to the hall of the slain by foxy female battle-maidens called Valkyrie.[26]

Or are you merely the wife of a mighty warrior? Sucks for you. The only way you can get to Valhalla is by suicide: you'll have to leap upon your valiant hubby's funeral pyre.

---

26. And yes, they're probably sporting braided pigtails and horned helmets.

What it's like: Crazy awesome. Valhalla has a roof made of overlapping shields and boasts 540 doors. Each door is so big that 800 warriors can walk through side-by-side. Every day, a rooster named Gullinkambi will wake these warriors up, and they'll spend all day in happy combat with each other. At the end of the day, all their wounds heal up—there's no death in Valhalla, and hopefully no pain either—and then the spirit warriors feast on boar, get sloppy drunk on mead served by lovely Valkyries, and then fall asleep. When Gullinkambi crows again, it's back to the fightin'. This helps them keep their combat skills sharp and their muscles toned. It continues until their services are needed for Ragnarok, the final apocalyptic battle in which the entire universe will be destroyed.

Surprise: A rainbow bridge connects Valhalla to earth. Seriously. A rainbow bridge. Keep an eye out for Care Bears

The Yellow Springs

What it is: The vaguely described land of the dead according to ancient Chinese folk religion.

Where it is: Beneath the earth.

How to get there: The ancient Chinese believed people had two complementary souls, the *hun* and the *p'o*. When you died, the *hun* escaped into the universe and became a divine ancestor. The *p'o*— which was thought to be yellow in color—followed the body into the ground, where it made its way to the Yellow Springs.

What it's like: For most people, not fun. Your soul has to perform heavy labor for the bureaucratic administrators of the underworld, which reflects the hierarchy of the world above. So if you were a poor, mistreated servant while you were alive, you would be poor and mistreated while dead.

Surprise: To keep the mistreatment to a minimum in the Yellow Springs, your relatives may have stocked your tomb with help-ful articles of clothing, money, food, and even human and animal servants—who would have been cremated after you died so they could join you. You should probably use the money to tip your ser-vants well in the afterlife. It's your fault they've been sent there, and they are *so* not thrilled about the arrangement.

CHAPTER 5

The Bible on Heaven
(A Scriptural Tour of Glory)

There are two big elephants in the room when it comes to the Western perspective on the afterlife, and both come from the Christian religious tradition: heaven and hell. So the *Pocket Guide* takes a break from its world religions focus to spend this chapter and the next in the Bible—presumably the source of our info on the two main destinations.

Let's take the good news first. First stop? Heaven.

As far as ideas go, the Christian concept of heaven is a tough one to grasp. According to the biblical account, it's a place filled with the presence of God and lit by the dazzling brightness of his glory. It's a place where sickness has been banished, where sin is absent, where sorrow is no more. It's a place of healing and goodness and eternal bliss.

How can finite humans even begin to comprehend it? This is how: By replacing the glory and light and presence with puffy white clouds, and dull blonde angels wearing white robes, and twinkly harp music, and rainbows. By taking the most profound idea in Western philosophy and turning it into the lamest place possible.

There are two main words in the Bible that get translated into the English words "heaven" or "heavens." They are *samayim* and *ouranos.*

SAMAYIM

A Hebrew term occurring more than three hundred times in the Old Testament. It's generally used to indicate everything in the natural world that was above the ground (the "earth"), as in the famous first verse of Genesis: "In the beginning, God created the heavens and the earth" (Genesis 1:1). A number of passages speak of "the heavens" not necessarily as the place you go when you die, but instead as the home of birds and stars and rain. It's just a longer, churchier word for *sky.*

But it's not quite that simple, because to the Old Testament authors, the heavens are more than just the sky. Some uses of *samayim* speak of it as the place where God lives (see Deuteronomy 26:15 and 2 Chronicles 30:27). The book of Job describes God holding court in the "heights of heaven" (Job 22:12). The Psalmist tells of the glory of the Almighty having been set "above the heavens" (Psalm 8:1) and proclaims that God is to be "exalted above the heavens" (Psalm 108:5). So the *samayim* wasn't just a place where the moon hung and the stars shone, but a created place where God lives, and where he spread out his glory, and where he was to be worshipped.

There's just one minor problem, for the *Pocket Guide*'s purposes. Despite the three hundred appearances of *samayim* in the Old Testament, we're hard-pressed to find any passages that indicate it's an eternal destination. Despite it being God's home, the Jewish people didn't necessarily view "the heavens" as a place for people to go after they die. Instead, the Hebrews thought they ended up in a shadowy place called *Sheol*. (See pp. 158–161 in the next chapter for more about *Sheol*.) *Sheol* was underground. It was the grave. It was conspicuously harp-free.

OURANOS

No harps in the New Testament, either, though the idea of heaven broadens a little there. The Greek word *ouranos* appears 269 times. For the most part, New Testament mentions of heaven match up with those used in the Old Testament. It's a replacement word for "sky" (Mark 13:25 describes stars "falling from heaven"), and it's also the place where God dwells (see Mark 16:19 below).

Like the Old Testament, not every use of *ouranos* is about an eternal destination. The Gospel of Matthew keeps mentioning something called "the kingdom of heaven," a phrase that appears thirty-two times in that book alone. This is where theologians start to split hairs and talk about "nuance" and heave up dramatic sighs when in the presence of the common pew-sitter. Why? Because most regular evangelical Christians read the phrase "kingdom of heaven," zero in on the word *heaven,* and automatically assume it's a reference to the Pearly Gates. But scholars and theologians? Not so fast, Jethro. Most of these guys are pretty certain "kingdom of heaven" isn't so much a reference to heaven as it is another way to say "kingdom of God," like the rest of the Gospels. And while the kingdom of God does have a blissful, future-y component, it also has a present-day meaning. It describes the entirety of the world under the control of the Almighty and subject to his will—whether it's the current world or some kind of world to come. Which means "kingdom of heaven" might have something to do with the Great Beyond, but not exclusively.

Confused? Join the club.

WHAT DOES THE BIBLE SAY?

So here's the situation. The Bible talks a lot about heaven—to the tune of 569 appearances of the translated word itself—but other than some passages in Revelation, very few of these seem to match up with the modern idea of where Christian believers go when they die. Most of the Old Testament *heaven*s are about the sky or God's dwelling place. Same goes for the New Testament, with a little "kingdom of heaven" mixed in. It can get repetitive. The *Pocket Guide* refuses to subject you to all that repetition, so here are a few arbitrarily selected highlights. Consider the following a divine sampler of the most heavenly parts of the Old and New Testaments.

☀ Genesis 7:11–12[1]

In the six hundredth year of Noah's life, on the seventeenth day of the second month—on that day all the springs of the great deep burst forth, and the floodgates of the heavens were opened. And rain fell on the earth forty days and forty nights.

---

1. Unless indicated otherwise, all quotations are from the New International Version (NIV) of the Bible.

What we learn: Heaven is used here in the "sky" sense, and it has floodgates. Or windows. And a lot of water.

Questions/comments: Probably metaphorical floodgates. Also? Noah was really old.

🌱 Deuteronomy 26:15

Look down from heaven, your holy dwelling place, and bless your people Israel and the land you have given us as you promised on oath to our forefathers, a land flowing with milk and honey.

What we learn: God dwells in heaven, and he's in a position to "look down" toward his people while blessing them, so location-wise, it must be up.

Questions/comments: Unless it's metaphorically "up."

🌱 1 Kings 8:30

Hear the supplication of your servant and of your people Israel when they pray toward this place. Hear from heaven, your dwelling place, and when you hear, forgive.

What we learn: God can hear people on earth even from all the way in heaven, and it results in forgiveness.

Questions/comments: Don't worry about keeping it down.

🌱 2 Kings 2:11

As they were walking along and talking together, suddenly a chariot of fire and horses of fire appeared and separated the two of them, and Elijah went up to heaven in a whirlwind.

What we learn: One of the only places in the Old Testament where heaven is treated as a destination. And one way, apparently, to get there? A tornado. And flaming chariots. Pulled by fire-horses.

Questions/comments: If fiery beasts take you to heaven, what in *samayim* takes you to hell?

⚜ 2 Chronicles 30:27

The priests and the Levites stood to bless the people, and God heard them, for their prayer reached heaven, his holy dwelling place.

What we learn: God can definitely hear your prayers in heaven.

Questions/comments: Odd how the author makes a point to say the priests' prayers "reached heaven" . . . as if there were the possibility that they might not?

⚜ Nehemiah 9:16

You give life to everything, and the multitudes of heaven worship you.

What we learn: Someone else is in heaven besides God.

Questions/comments: Besides Elijah, who exactly are these inhabitants? Angels? Departed souls?

⚜ Psalm 11:4

The LORD is in his holy temple; / the LORD is on his heavenly throne. / He observes the sons of men; / his eyes examine them.

What we learn: God sits on a throne and is watching . . .

Questions/comments: Better stop that.

⚜ Isaiah 66:1

This is what the LORD says: / "Heaven is my throne, / and the earth is my footstool. / Where is the house you will build for me? / Where will my resting place be?"

What we learn: If the universe is like a living room, then heaven is God's chair and the earth is where he rests his feet. And he's, um, waiting for mankind to build him a house?

Questions/comments: Apocalyptic poetry is hard.[2]

---

2. The rest of the heavenly shout-outs in the Old Testament are pretty much variations on these previous "heavenly throne" and/or "the heavens" themes. Let's skip ahead to the New Testament, where heaven gets a little more interesting.

> "... she went on and told me all about the good place. She said all a
> body would have to do there was to go around all day long with a harp
> and sing, forever and ever. So I didn't think much of it ... I asked her if she
> reckoned Tom Sawyer would go there, and she said not by a considerable
> sight. I was glad about that, because I wanted him and me to be together."
>
> (Huck Finn in *The Adventures of Huckleberry Finn*, by Mark Twain)

☀ Matthew 5:3

Blessed are the poor in spirit, for theirs is the kingdom of heaven.

What we learn: One of the first uses of "kingdom of heaven,"
which isn't necessarily the place you go when you die. At any rate, it
belongs to and will be populated by the downcast.

Questions/comments: Hopefully being in heaven (eventually)
will cheer them up a little.

☀ Matthew 5:11–12

*Blessed are you when people insult you, persecute you and falsely say all kinds of
evil against you because of me. Rejoice and be glad, because great is your reward
in heaven, for in the same way they persecuted the prophets who were before you.*

What we learn: Those who are persecuted for their faith will be
rewarded richly in heaven, like the prophets of old.

Questions/comments: But probably not "rewarded" in the
harem-of-virgins sense.

☀ Matthew 6:20

*But store up for yourselves treasures in heaven, where moth and rust do not
destroy, and where thieves do not break in and steal.*

What we learn: The treasures you store in heaven are eternal,
not temporary.

Questions/comments: Heaven has a good security system.

Matthew 7:21

Not everyone who says to me, "Lord, Lord," will enter the kingdom of heaven, but only he who does the will of my Father who is in heaven.

What we learn: It's not enough to just throw Jesus' name around. Your place in heaven has something to do with obedience when it comes to the will of God.

Questions/comments: "Kingdom of heaven" is used here, but this verse is referenced all the time—especially among conservative evangelicals—as having to do with gaining access to the Pearly Gates.

☀ **Matthew 8:11–12**

I say to you that many will come from the east and the west, and will take their places at the feast with Abraham, Isaac and Jacob in the kingdom of heaven. But the subjects of the kingdom will be thrown outside, into the darkness, where there will be weeping and gnashing of teeth.

What we learn: The "kingdom of heaven" is like a dinner party with interesting companions, if you can ignore the poor souls outside who didn't get invited.

Questions/comments: Dining with the Patriarchs sounds good, but the teeth-gnashing outside the doors could get distracting.

☀ **Matthew 10:32–33**

Whoever acknowledges me before men, I will also acknowledge him before my Father in heaven. But whoever disowns me before men, I will disown him before my Father in heaven.

What we learn: If Jesus is heaven's gatekeeper, it's best to get to know him sooner rather than later.

Questions/comments: Maybe this "acknowledging" has to do with doing the will of God, as already mentioned in Matthew 7:21.

☀ **Matthew 12:50**

For whoever does the will of my Father in heaven is my brother and sister and mother.

What we learn: Jesus may have a really big family.

Questions/comments: At least, that's what the *Pocket Guide* hopes.

✹ Matthew 18:10

See that you do not look down on one of these little ones. For I tell you that their angels in heaven always see the face of my Father in heaven.

What we learn: Apparently, children have their own personal angels, to whom God's face is always visible.

Questions/comments: If the whole sweet little guardian angels thing is true, a lot of people are gonna be really embarrassed once they meet their angels in heaven. Because you know what they saw? *Everything.*

✹ Mark 13:31

Heaven and earth will pass away, but my words will never pass away.

What we learn: Wait—heaven is not eternal? Or is it the starry "heavens" that aren't eternal?

Questions/comments: Neither option is very encouraging.

✹ Mark 16:19

After the Lord Jesus had spoken to them, he was taken up into heaven and he sat at the right hand of God.

What we learn: At the Ascension, Jesus went up. And sat down next to God.

Questions/comments: This means heaven has furniture of some sort. In the *Pocket Guide*'s imagination, it's either clear—like glass—or super-duper blingy. Like what would happen if a tornado tore through a strip mall containing a jewelry store, a throne warehouse, and a glue factory.

✹ Luke 6:23

Blessed are you when men hate you, when they exclude you and insult you and reject your name as evil, because of the Son of Man. Rejoice in that

> *"Simultaneous with my last recollection of seeing the bridge and the rain, a light enveloped me, with a brilliance beyond earthly comprehension or description. . . . In my next moment of awareness, I was standing in heaven."*
>
> (Don Piper in *90 Minutes in Heaven*, 2004)

day and leap for joy, because great is your reward in heaven. For that is how their fathers treated the prophets.

What we learn: Persecution on earth will result in some kind of happy reward in heaven.

Questions/comments: It's one thing to look forward to a post-life reward for hardship, but actually leaping for joy about suffering? That's a lot to ask. Especially for elderly believers whose physicians have asked them to refrain from unnecessary physical exertion.

☀ Luke 10:20

However, do not rejoice that the spirits submit to you, but rejoice that your names are written in heaven.

What we learn: People's names are written in heaven, perhaps in the "Lamb's Book of Life" (Revelation 20:15—see p. 152).

Questions/comments: John Smith? You're in luck.

☀ Luke 15:7

I tell you that in the same way there will be more rejoicing in heaven over one sinner who repents than over ninety-nine righteous persons who do not need to repent.

What we learn: Nothing's more interesting to heaven than that wonderful moment when a sinner finds God.

141

Questions/comments: Nothing's less interesting to heaven than a self-righteous blowhard who *thinks* he's found God.

🌿 Luke 20:34–36

Jesus replied, "The people of this age marry and are given in marriage. But those who are considered worthy of taking part in that age and in the resurrection from the dead will neither marry nor be given in marriage, and they can no longer die; for they are like the angels. They are God's children, since they are children of the resurrection."

What we learn: No being married, getting married, or proposing marriage in heaven. No death in heaven either. Resurrected life is eternal and supernatural, even angelic.

Questions/comments: You know that old idea that you get wings and a harp when you enter heaven? The part about being "like the angels" is probably where it comes from.

🌿 John 3:12–13

I have spoken to you of earthly things and you do not believe; how then will you believe if I speak of heavenly things? No one has ever gone into heaven except the one who came from heaven—the Son of Man.

What we learn: No one has gone to heaven yet, according to Jesus. And if anyone would know . . .

Questions/comments: Jesus and the *Pocket Guide*'s Sunday school teachers seriously need to get on the same page here, because somebody's spreading some inaccurate information. In this case, the *Pocket Guide* sides with Jesus. "Always side with Jesus" being a good rule of thumb in almost every situation.

🌿 John 14:2–3

In my Father's house are many rooms; if it were not so, I would have told you. I am going there to prepare a place for you. And if I go and prepare a place for you, I will come back and take you to be with me that you also may be where I am.

What we learn: Heaven is like a big house with lots of rooms, and Jesus is setting out the chocolate mints and guest linens.

Questions/comments: If heaven is a house, what does that do to the "streets of gold"? Are they more like hallways?

☀ Acts 1:9–11

After he said this, he was taken up before their very eyes, and a cloud hid him from their sight. They were looking intently up into the sky as he was going, when suddenly two men dressed in white stood beside them. "Men of Galilee," they said, "why do you stand here looking into the sky? This same Jesus, who has been taken from you into heaven, will come back in the same way you have seen him go into heaven."

What we learn: When Jesus went to heaven, he traveled upward. It wouldn't hurt to keep your eyes peeled that way, too, because he's coming back from the same direction.

Questions/comments: Weird detail about the cloud that "hid him from their sight." Is it metaphor? Misdirection? Convenient meteorology?

☀ Acts 2:29,34

Brothers, I can tell you confidently that the patriarch David died and was buried, and his tomb is here to this day. For David did not ascend to heaven . . .

What we learn: More than a thousand years after David probably died, Peter says that the great Hebrew king bought it physically— and while trusting in God's promises—but his body has not yet been resurrected.

Questions/comments: Scholars date the writing of Acts in the first century, at which point David hadn't yet "gone to heaven" in a physical sense. What about the twenty-first century? Is he there yet? How long does it take? And why do Don Piper and all those near-death experience people go there immediately if King David has to deal with a multi-thousand-year waiting period?

☀ Acts 7:56

But Stephen, full of the Holy Spirit, looked up to heaven and saw the glory of God, and Jesus standing at the right hand of God. "Look," he said, "I see heaven open and the Son of Man standing at the right hand of God."

What we learn: Heaven is capable of "opening up." And according to Stephen's vision—which so angers his listeners that they immediately execute him for blasphemy—Jesus is *standing* in heaven next to God. Not sitting, as in Mark 16:19.

Questions/comments: "Opening up" . . . like curtains? Like a window? Like a door? Like floodgates?

☀ Romans 1:18–19

The wrath of God is being revealed from heaven against all the godlessness and wickedness of men who suppress the truth by their wickedness, since what may be known about God is plain to them, because God has made it plain to them.

What we learn: Heaven looks a lot better when you're full of the Holy Spirit, like Stephen. In the previous verse, he looks up to heaven and sees the glory of God. The godless and wicked? They get a heavenly eyeful of wrath.

Questions/comments: Another good rule of thumb, in addition to the siding-with-Jesus rule? Don't be wicked.

☀ 2 Corinthians 12:2–3

I know a man in Christ who fourteen years ago was caught up to the third heaven. Whether it was in the body or out of the body I do not know—God

144

knows. And I know that this man . . . was caught up to paradise. He heard inexpressible things, things that man is not permitted to tell.

What we learn: There's something called the "third heaven" that seems to be a combination of paradise and an out-of-body experience where one might hear inexpressible things. Unless Paul's just taking an opportunity to be all mysterious and poetic.

Questions/comments: If the sky is the first heaven, and God's dwelling place is the second heaven, then what's the third heaven? And what exactly would a person hear there? And why in the world does Paul tantalize his readers by bringing up these "inexpressible things" but refusing to explain what they are? Such a metaphysical tease, this guy.

✖ **Philippians 3:20–21**

But our citizenship is in heaven. And we eagerly await a Savior from there, the Lord Jesus Christ, who, by the power that enables him to bring everything under his control, will transform our lowly bodies so that they will be like his glorious body.

What we learn: Jesus will change our earthly bodies into glorious heavenly bodies more befitting the place where we are citizens.

Questions/comments: Define *glorious,* please. Does it mean shiny? Transparent? Acne-free? Better-toned? And how old will these Jesus-like bodies be? Because some people look a lot more glorious in their twenties than they do at thirty-three, the age Jesus departed his earthly body.

✖ **1 Peter 3:21–22**

. . . and this water symbolizes baptism that now saves you also—not the removal of dirt from the body but the pledge of a good conscience toward

God. It saves you by the resurrection of Jesus Christ, who has gone into heaven and is at God's right hand—with angels, authorities and powers in submission to him.

What we learn: Not only is Jesus sitting to the right of God in heaven, but he's got some clout there. He's in charge of angels, and authorities, and "powers."

Questions/comments: In this context, "powers" probably refers to supernatural beings. As opposed to the kinds of powers you might see displayed by a guy in a cape.

2 Peter 3:13

But in keeping with his promise we are looking forward to a new heaven and a new earth, the home of righteousness.

What we learn: In the last days, the idea of a "new earth" is tied into the idea of heaven. Both will be considered places of righteousness, and probably have something to do with the Gospels' "kingdom of heaven" a.k.a. the "kingdom of God."

Questions/comments: Will there be mosquitoes in the new earth? Because if ever there was a time to get rid of those suckers . . .

1 Thessalonians 4:16–17

For the Lord himself will come down from heaven, with a loud command, with the voice of the archangel and with the trumpet call of God, and the dead in Christ will rise first. After that, we who are still alive and are left will be caught up together with them in the clouds to meet the Lord in the air. And so we will be with the Lord forever.

What we learn: At some point Jesus will descend from heaven with a shout and trumpet accompaniment, and the physical resurrection will follow. The already-dead and the living will be "caught up . . . in the clouds to meet the Lord in the air." When

146

taken literally, this description sounds kinda freaky. So it means different things to different people, generally depending on how many *Left Behind* books they've read.[3]

Questions/comments: Wanna boost your YouTube hits? Hang out near a church cemetery when the "dead in Christ" rise first, and bring your camcorder.

☀ 2 Thessalonians 1:6–7

God is just: He will pay back trouble to those who trouble you and give relief to you who are troubled, and to us as well. This will happen when the Lord Jesus is revealed from heaven in blazing fire with his powerful angels.

What we learn: There's fire—blazing fire—in heaven, too, and you'll see it when Jesus makes an appearance out of heaven. Even better, this is when your enemies will get what's coming.

---

3. 1 Thessalonians 4:17 is the biblical cornerstone of those who believe in the Rapture—the idea that believers will be physically lifted skyward, into heaven, prior to the Second Coming. It's also the source of some spectacularly campy scenes in evangelistic films from the 1970s.

Questions/comments: Jesus being revealed from heaven with a posse of angels is dramatic enough. The pyrotechnics may be overkill.

✿ Hebrews 11:16

Instead, they were longing for a better country—a heavenly one. Therefore God is not ashamed to be called their God, for he has prepared a city for them.

What we learn: Heaven is like a country. No wait, it's like a city. No wait . . .

Questions/comments: If anything, maybe heaven heals the deepening urban/rural divide.

✿ Hebrews 12:22–23

But you have come to Mount Zion, to the heavenly Jerusalem, the city of the living God. You have come to thousands upon thousands of angels in joyful assembly, to the church of the firstborn, whose names are written in heaven. You have come to God, the judge of all men, to the spirits of righteous men made perfect. . . .

What we learn: No, heaven is more like a mountain—specifically, Mount Zion. But it's still kind of like a city, too. Anyway, it's home to a whole lot of angels, along with the perfected spirits of believers.

Questions/comments: The author of Hebrews is having a difficult time describing heaven. It's very Don Piper–like.[4]

✿ James 3:17

But the wisdom that comes from heaven is first of all pure; then peace-loving, considerate, submissive, full of mercy and good fruit, impartial and sincere.

---

4. See p. 93 in Chapter 3.

148

What we learn: Thinking heavenly thoughts leads to good personal qualities.

Questions/comments: Impartial wisdom and considerate sincerity are great qualities in, for instance, a federal judge. As long as he plays it cool. Such a judge wouldn't want to be too vocal about where he scored his judicial fruit.

☀ Revelation 7:9

After this I looked and there before me was a great multitude that no one could count, from every nation, tribe, people and language, standing before the throne and in front of the Lamb. They were wearing white robes and were holding palm branches in their hands.

What we learn: Heaven is multi-culti, packed full with all races and ethnicities of people.

Questions/comments: Unfortunately, the fashion options will be far less diverse than the inhabitants.

☀ Revelation 7:16–17

Never again will they hunger; never again will they thirst. The sun will not beat upon them, nor any scorching heat. For the Lamb at the center of the throne will be their shepherd; he will lead them to springs of living water. And God will wipe away every tear from their eyes.

What we learn: You won't be hungry in heaven. You won't be thirsty in heaven. You won't get sunburned in heaven or even get too hot. Also, no crying, thanks to the Lamb.

Questions/comments: Just FYI, it's not a fluffy cute lamb with big dewy eyes and a bunch of woodland creatures as his companions. It's a bloody, raw lamb that has been slain.[5] Also? It's Jesus.

---

5. See Revelation 5:6. And not only is it a mutilated lamb, but it also has seven horns and seven eyes, each of which is symbolic. Revelation digs the metaphor.

❋ Revelation 21:1-3

Then I saw a new heaven and a new earth, for the first heaven and the first earth had passed away, and there was no longer any sea. I saw the Holy City, the new Jerusalem, coming down out of heaven from God, prepared as a bride beautifully dressed for her husband. And I heard a loud voice from the throne saying, "Now the dwelling of God is with men, and he will live with them. They will be his people, and God himself will be with them and be their God. . . ."

What we learn: Heaven as it is now will eventually cease to exist, only to be replaced with a new heaven, which has something to do with a new earth. And instead of people going to be with God in heaven, it sounds as if God will bring heaven down to earth to dwell with his people.[6]

Questions/comments: Interesting, then, how Christians always talk about "going to heaven," when it sure reads as if heaven comes to them.

❋ Revelation 21:4

He will wipe every tear from their eyes. There will be no more death or mourning or crying or pain, for the old order of things has passed away.

What we learn: Things like crying and pain and death and sadness are absolutely not a part of heaven. That's the old way of things. Welcome to the new.

---

6. From this point, the rest of the verses about heaven aren't talking about the traditional "going to be with God" idea of heaven, but rather the "new heaven" and "new earth" spoken of here. Most Christians don't ever distinguish between the two—and probably have never really thought much about it—but theologians like N. T. Wright are trying to change that. See his provocative book *Surprised by Hope: Rethinking Heaven, the Resurrection, and the Mission of the Church* (San Francisco: HarperOne, 2008).

> *"Surely it is not wrong for us to think and talk about Heaven. I like to find out all I can about it. I expect to live there through all eternity. If I were going to dwell in any place in this country, if I were going to make it my home, I would inquire about its climate, about the neighbors I would have—about everything, in fact, that I could learn concerning it. . . . We are going to spend eternity in another world. . . . Is it not natural that we should look and listen and try to find out who is already there and what is the route to take?"*
>
> (Dwight L. Moody in *The D. L. Moody Year Book*, 1900)

Questions/comments: Laughs aside, the *Pocket Guide* can get behind that.

✹ Revelation 21:15

The angel who talked with me had a measuring rod of gold to measure the city, its gates and its walls. The city was laid out like a square, as long as it was wide. He measured the city with the rod and found it to be 12,000 stadia in length, and as wide and high as it is long.

What we learn: Heaven is shaped like a cube, somewhere in the vicinity of 1,400 miles wide, long, and high. That's a really big cube.[7]

Questions/comments: If you Google "cube" and "heaven," you get a lot of links to the song, "Heaven," by the rapper Ice Cube. Its lyrics explain very little about this passage.

✹ Revelation 21:21

The twelve gates were twelve pearls, each gate made of a single pearl. The great street of the city was of pure gold, like transparent glass.

---

7. Ancient people thought that the cube was the most perfect shape ever. So a cube-shaped heaven may just be a metaphorical comment on its physical perfection.

What we learn: Pearly gates. Streets of gold. This is where it comes from.

Questions/comments: That's one honking big pearl.

✹ Revelation 21:23

The city does not need the sun or the moon to shine on it, for the glory of God gives it light, and the Lamb is its lamp.

What we learn: Heaven will not be illuminated by lesser objects like the sun or moon, but by God himself.

Questions/comments: Compact fluorescents have nothing on the extended bulb life of, well, *God.*

✹ Revelation 21:27

Nothing impure will ever enter it, nor will anyone who does what is shameful or deceitful, but only those whose names are written in the Lamb's book of life.

What we learn: No heaven crashers. No shameful or deceitful people, either. Only those with legit reservations get in . . .

Questions/comments: . . . including John Smith.

✹ Revelation 22:1

Then the angel showed me the river of the water of life, as clear as crystal, flowing from the throne of God and of the Lamb down the middle of the great street of the city. On each side of the river stood the tree of life, bearing twelve crops of fruit, yielding its fruit every month. And the leaves of the tree are for the healing of the nations.

What we learn: Heaven has at least one river and a multi-fruit tree, which ought to please the vegan inhabitants of heaven. Fishermen, too.

Questions/comments: That multicrop fruit-vending tree is a great idea. The *Pocket Guide* sorta wishes God hadn't saved that one for himself.

152

CHAPTER 6

The Bible on Hell
A Holy Trek Through the Fiery Pit

ow for the bad news. Heaven is wonderful, but it has its less idyllic counterpart: hell. If you're like most members of Western culture, you probably have a pretty good mental picture of hell. After all, hell finds its way into all kinds of daily conversations. Most people are so familiar with it they use it as a common standard of comparison. English-speakers have decided that quite a few things—like summer temperatures, or jalapeno peppers, or certain celebrities—are hotter than hell. Many tasks are hard as hell. Chaotic events and/or insane ex-spouses may be crazy as hell. Inexplicably, some winter days are as cold as hell.

That's interesting. Interesting as hell, in fact. And in the typical Western mind, hell *is* a pretty interesting place once you can get past the everlasting torment. Based on tradition, folk wisdom, and the profound insight of the Gary Larson oeuvre,[1] this is what the Christian hell is apparently like:

 It is physically warm, as in "on fire." Skin-scorching hot, with rivers of magma and explosions of flame and, for good measure, fountains of Tabasco sauce.

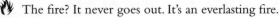 It is filled with sinners, who are also on fire.

The fire? It never goes out. It's an everlasting fire.

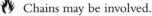 The sinners? They never die, but are tormented forever and ever for their sins.

Chains may be involved.

There's a lot of red lighting, and smoke, and the occasional scream of torment.

Satan is there, clad in a skintight red jumpsuit, holding a pitch-fork or trident, sporting a pointy goatee and prancing around with his little horns and goat feet.

Demons are there, too. And they're scary, but their official responsibilities are hazy. Perhaps they crack whips and stoke the fires?

The eternal physical torture is bad and everything, but the worst thing about hell—according to Christian tradition—is that God is *not* there.

---

1. The guy who created *The Far Side* and contributed a generous number of classic cartoons about hell, including the one where the Devil is leading a torturous aerobics class.

HELLUVA JOB, DANTE

A few critics, though, are fond of suggesting that these hellish characteristics owe a whole lot more to classic literature (Milton, Dante, Bill Weise) than to anything found in the Bible. For example, neither the Old nor the New Testament offers much detail about Satan—whether in regard to his tights, color palette, or preferences in facial hair—but Milton's *Paradise Lost* helpfully fleshes out the character in great detail. Meanwhile, Dante introduced the world to the workaday activities of hell in the "Inferno" section of his *Divine Comedy,* with its sadistic-yet-colorful accounts of horror and suffering. For instance, Dante's nine circles of hell were populated by blasphemers (who were eternally pelted by flames), corrupt politicians (whom he saw boiling in oil), and "sowers of discord" (who experienced perpetual mutilation-then-healing-then-mutilation-again at the hands of sword-wielding demons, who were devilishly happy to lop off their victims' limbs, disgorge their entrails, and cleave their bodies from the chin all the way down to the place "where one breaketh wind").[2]

The question the *Pocket Guide* wants answered, though, is not *What do we learn about hell from college literature courses?* Nope. A better question is *What does the Bible say?* Hell is supposed to be a concept originating in Christianity. So do the Christian Scriptures mention all those hellish details?

---

2. Yes, that's the particular fate of the Islamic prophet Muhammad, whose entrails are seen hanging down between his legs. The "breaketh wind" phrase comes from line 24 of Henry Wadsworth Longfellow's classic English translation (1865) of Dante's Inferno, Canto XXVIII. See pp. 185–186 in the next chapter for more about Dante and the creative punishments of hell.

Easy answer: Um, not exactly.

But that's not the complete answer. First, a quick lesson in biblical linguistics.

A Quick Lesson in Biblical Linguistics

The Bible was originally written in Hebrew (the Old Testament) and Greek (the New Testament), with a little Aramaic thrown in for good measure. In these languages, four different words have, in certain versions of the Bible, been translated into the English word *hell*. Unfortunately, these translations—though influential (cough, cough, *King James*)—aren't always accurate.

Sheol: The all-purpose Hebrew term for the grave, the place of the dead, or the dark netherworld. Location-wise, it was generally thought to be downward, or beneath the earth. It was a quiet, shadowy place, but otherwise void of much else in the way of detail. The earlier books of the Old Testament (including the Pentateuch[3] as well as Psalms, Ecclesiastes, and Job) seem to indicate that everybody goes to *Sheol*—the just and the unjust, the righteous and the unrighteous, murderers and priests, gay male prostitutes and Baptist deacons. *Sheol* appears sixty-five times in the Old Testament. In the King James Version, it's translated thirty-one times as "hell," thirty-one times as "the grave," and just to keep things fresh, three times it becomes "the pit."

Contemporary scholarship thinks King James missed the boat on this one. It tends to view *Sheol* as a completely different

---

3. The first five books of the Old Testament: Genesis, Exodus, Leviticus, Numbers, and Deuteronomy. Also known as "the Hebrew Bible," though "Pentateuch" rolls off the tongue better in a pleasingly Germanic way.

concept from the fire-and-brimstone hell. *Sheol* is not a place. *Sheol* doesn't involve punishment. It's just a poetic way of talking about death, or nothingness. The New International Version—which happens to be the translation preferred by the *Pocket Guide*—generally uses "the grave" as the English equivalent of *Sheol,* as in "Like sheep they are destined for the grave, / death will feed on them" (Psalm 49:14).[4] In the NIV, the word *hell* doesn't show up until the New Testament.

By the way, the belief that the afterlife was divided into opposite destinations, a heaven and hell, didn't really develop until later in Jewish history, sometime after the Babylonian Exile and a few centuries prior to the time of Christ. The noncanonical Book of Enoch, thought to have been written in 160 B.C.E., splits *Sheol* into multiple sections. These include one for the righteous who are awaiting Judgment and another for the wicked, who undergo punishment while they wait to be judged. (Blame it on Zoroaster.[5])

Hades: The Greek version of *Sheol. Hades* is the Greek word used in the New Testament to refer to the dwelling place of the dead, and even appears as a stand-in for *Sheol* in the Septuagint, a Greek translation of the Old Testament. For kicks and giggles, compare the English Standard Version's translation of Psalm 16:10 ("you will not abandon my soul to Sheol") with Peter's quotation of Psalm 16:10 in Acts 2:27 NIV ("you will not abandon my soul to Hades"). Note that neither usage implies sinners being tortured by fire or mauled by demons.

Hades appears eleven times in the New Testament. The King James Version translates it "the grave" once and "hell" the other ten

---

4. In these cases, the NIV gets all scholarly and attaches a footnote to "grave." The footnote usually reads "Hebrew *Sheol.*"

5. See pp. 48–49 in Chapter 2.

times. The New International Version uses "hell" or "the depths," but always with a footnote tying it to *Hades*.

Depending on your moral disposition, the usage of *Sheol* and *Hades* is either good news or bad. Because already two of the four words traditionally thought to refer to "hell" probably aren't about hell at all. They're just about plain old death.

Tartaroo: By far the silliest way to talk about hell, *Tartaroo* is a Greek word used only once in the Bible, in 2 Peter 2:4. It's a reference to Tartarus, the dungeon-like underworld in Greek mythology devoted to suffering and torment. Most translations call this one "hell," and based on the context of the verse itself (keep reading), this version of hell seems to apply only to the residence of demons.

Gehenna: This is the hell you'd do well to avoid. The Greek word *gehenna* doesn't just refer to some generalized state of being dead, but to an actual state of being tormented on account of your having been evil. But, as might be expected, it's a little more complicated than it first appears. *Gehenna* is Greek, but it's based on a Hebrew word: *Ge-Hinnom,* otherwise known as the Hinnom Valley, which gets a few biblical shout-outs in places like Joshua 18:16. The Hinnom Valley wasn't exactly a happy place, known in the Old Testament as a site where children were slaughtered in ritual sacrifices to the pagan god Molech. By the time Jesus came around, this valley was a garbage dump outside Jerusalem. And guess what? It was always on fire. Trash got tossed in there to be consumed, along with animal carcasses and the bodies of criminals. It was a very real, very physical place with a chilling history, and it made a nice reference point for Jesus to talk about what would happen to sinners after they died.

Gehenna appears twelve times in the New Testament, mostly in the teachings of Jesus.

OK. Linguistics lesson over. Let's move on to the verses themselves. Which, you'll notice, highlight very few Old Testament mentions of hell. *Why,* you ask? Because most of them aren't hell at all. They're *Sheol.* Try to keep up.[6]

☙ Deuteronomy 32:22

For a fire has been kindled by my wrath, / one that burns to the realm of death below. / It will devour the earth and its harvests / and set afire the foundations of the mountains.

Word used: *Sheol*

What we learn: "The realm of death below" is a pretty standard use of *Sheol,* but the fire stuff is a bonus. It works pretty well with the traditional idea of hell. And the flames of this realm? They're fueled by God's wrath.

Questions/comments: Shudder.

☙ Numbers 16:33

They went down alive into the grave, with everything they owned; the earth closed over them, and they perished and were gone from the community.

Word used: *Sheol*

What we learn: The rebellious sons of Korah get swallowed up by the earth for rebelling against God and Moses. The King James translates this "the pit"—reinforcing the idea that hell is under the earth—but really it's just another use of "the grave."

---

6. The *Pocket Guide* will give you a few arbitrary instances of *Sheol* and Hades, then move into the more accurately hellish *Gehenna*s of the New Testament. There are plenty of additional *Sheol* appearances—62 of them, to be precise—but this chapter is about hell. Not the grave.

Questions/comments: Notice how the sons of Korah were sent to *Sheol* with their possessions. Apparently you *can* take it with you.

🌿 2 Samuel 22:6

The cords of the grave coiled around me; / the snares of death confronted me.
Word used: *Sheol*

What we learn: In a song of praise, David sings these words while trying to escape from Saul. It's clear he's talking metaphorically about death, because he's using a parallelism—a Hebrew linguistic trick that applies two phrases in description of one subject. The tricky sentence construction is too much for the King James Version, which turns the "cords of the grave" into the far scarier "sorrows of hell."

Questions/comments: Obviously, King James thought parallelisms were stupid.

🌿 Daniel 12:2

Multitudes who sleep in the dust of the earth will awake: some to everlasting life, others to shame and everlasting contempt.

What we learn: A lot. Suddenly, resurrection out of *Sheol*—a brand-new idea in Judaism—becomes a possibility, thanks to this book written during the Babylonian Exile. But there's another option, too. If you don't awake to everlasting life? Your eternal alarm clock buzzes with "shame and everlasting contempt," which seems a wee bit more hell-ish than *Sheol*-ish. And because you probably think of hell as being a physically painful place, observe that it also rocks the mental torment.

Questions/comments: Poor self-esteem now? Just wait until that "everlasting contempt" shows up to punch your psyche in the eye.

162

> *"The God that holds you over the pit of hell, much as one holds a spider, or some loathsome insect over the fire, abhors you, and is dreadfully provoked: His wrath towards you burns like fire."*
>
> (Puritan preacher Jonathan Edwards in his famous 1741 sermon "Sinners in the Hands of an Angry God")

☀ Isaiah 33:14

The sinners in Zion are terrified; / trembling grips the godless: / "Who of us can dwell with the consuming fire? / Who of us can dwell with everlasting burning?"

What we learn: This verse—traditionally thought to describe hell on account of all the fire imagery—makes it clear that hell is a place of knee-knocking terror. Especially for the godless.

Questions/comments: "Consuming fire" and "everlasting burning" aren't exactly compatible with each other. So which is it?

☀ Malachi 4:1

"Surely the day is coming; it will burn like a furnace. All the arrogant and every evildoer will be stubble, and that day that is coming will set them on fire," says the LORD Almighty.

What we learn: A day of judgment is coming when evildoers will be set on fire. Not to be too matter-of-fact about it.

Questions/comments: The "set on fire" part earns this verse a traditional association with hell. Also, it makes the *Pocket Guide* think of those stunt guys on movie sets who, having inexplicably become engulfed in flames, end up running through scenes of devastation and chaos while flapping their fiery arms. Sigh. That's so wrong.

❋ Matthew 3:11–12

I baptize you with water for repentance. But after me will come one who is more powerful than I, whose sandals I am not fit to carry. He will baptize you with the Holy Spirit and with fire. His winnowing fork is in his hand, and he will clear his threshing floor, gathering his wheat into the barn and burning up the chaff with unquenchable fire.

What we learn: According to John the Baptist, the speaker in this passage, Jesus, will divide people according to the desirable (the edible wheat) and the trash (the inedible chaff). The trash is set ablaze.

Questions/comments: You'd be right in thinking that chaff ought to burn up almost immediately, but John says the fires of judgment won't snuff out.

❋ Matthew 5:22

But I tell you that anyone who is angry with his brother will be subject to judgment . . . anyone who says, 'You fool!' will be in danger of the fire of hell.

Word used: *Gehenna*

What we learn: Angry people and those who call others by contemptuous names—including "fool"—are in danger of hellfire.

Questions/comments: Mr. T is totally screwed.

❋ Matthew 10:28

Do not be afraid of those who kill the body but cannot kill the soul. Rather, be afraid of the One who can destroy both soul and body in hell.

Word used: *Gehenna*

What we learn: Murderers? Not so scary, because your soul will survive death. What's scary is how hell goes a step beyond. It doesn't just destroy your body. It destroys your soul, too.

164

"The images of hell that Sacred Scripture presents to us must be correctly interpreted. They show the complete frustration and emptiness of life without God. Rather than a place, hell indicates the state of those who freely and definitively separate themselves from God, the source of all life and joy."

(Pope John Paul II in a General Audience on July 28, 1999)

Questions/comments: Seems to be saying the torment of hell is not everlasting—eventually it ends with the destruction of the soul. Consuming Fire: 1. Everlasting Burning: 0.

Matthew 16:18

And I tell you that you are Peter, and on this rock I will build my church, and the gates of Hades will not overcome it.

Word used: *Hades*

What we learn: The grave, or death, or hell (if you're really hardcore) will not be able to defeat the church of Jesus. And it has something to do with the disciple Peter.

Questions/comments: This verse is a controversial one among Protestants and Catholics, based on who exactly is the "rock" being referred to here. Catholics say it's Peter—whose Greek name, *Petros,* means "stone"—which established him as the first in a long line of heads of the Church, otherwise known as the pope. Protestants don't buy into the whole papacy thing, so they figure the "rock" in question must be Jesus, talking about himself in the third person.

Matthew 25:41

Then he will say to those on his left, "Depart from me, you who are cursed, into the eternal fire prepared for the devil and his angels."

165

What we learn: Jesus again, and here he says the punishing fires of hell aren't just for the unrighteous, but also for the devil and his demons.

Questions/comments: Serves them right. And score one for "Everlasting Burning."

🌱 Matthew 25:46

Then they will go away to eternal punishment, but the righteous to eternal life.

What we learn: Jesus is still talking about those "who are cursed" or "those on his left." Based on earlier verses in the passage, these people are those who, unlike the righteous, failed to care for the needy. The result of their inaction? Eternal punishment.

Questions/comments: When was the last time you volunteered at the homeless shelter?

🌱 Mark 9:43–45

If your hand causes you to sin, cut it off. It is better for you to enter life maimed than with two hands to go into hell, where the fire never goes out. And if your foot causes you to sin, cut it off. It is better for you to enter life crippled than to have two feet and be thrown into hell. And if your eye causes you to sin, pluck it out.

Word used: *Gehenna*

What we learn: A person should probably do everything he or she can to steer clear of the everlasting fires of hell, even to the point of personal eye-gouging or dismemberment.

Questions/comments: Makes you wonder why more Christians aren't sporting eye-patches. Or peg-legs.

"There is no doctrine which I would more willingly remove from Christianity than [the doctrine of hell], if it lay in my power. But it has the full support of Scripture and, specially, of our Lord's own words; it has always been held by Christendom; and it has the support of reason."

(C. S. Lewis in *The Problem of Pain*, 1940)

☀ Mark 9:47–48

It is better for you to enter the kingdom of God with one eye than to have two eyes and be thrown into hell, where "their worm does not die, / and the fire is not quenched."

Word used: *Gehenna*

What we learn: The fires of hell are never quenched. Even worse, hell seems to be occupied by horrible death-proof worms.

Questions/comments: The worm is probably metaphorical. Jesus is quoting here from Isaiah 66:24, which refers to the rotting carcasses of men who rebelled against God. This is a case of the Greek word *gehenna* being translated "hell." Gehenna, the garbage dump south of Jerusalem, would have been full of burning trash and animal carcasses, which made it a pretty good habitat for maggots.

☀ Luke 16:19–24

There was a rich man who was dressed in purple and fine linen and lived in luxury every day. At his gate was laid a beggar named Lazarus, covered with sores and longing to eat what fell from the rich man's table. . . . The time came when the beggar died and the angels carried him to Abraham's side. The rich man also died and was buried. In hell, where he was in torment,

167

*he looked up and saw Abraham far away, with Lazarus by his side. So he
called to him, "Father Abraham, have pity on me and send Lazarus to dip
the tip of his finger in water and cool my tongue, because I am in agony in
this fire."*

Word used: *Hades*

What we learn: A lot. In this famous parable, Jesus reveals that
(1) a life of luxury doesn't keep you out of hell; (2) the rich guy is
in physical burning agony, not just the metaphorical kind; and (3)
apparently conversations can take place between people in hell and
people in heaven.[7] Which has to be awkward.

Questions/comments: Aim higher, rich man. A fingertip of
water isn't gonna help much with the suffering.

❧ Luke 16:25–26

*But Abraham replied, "Son, remember that in your lifetime you received
your good things, while Lazarus received bad things, but now he is comforted
here and you are in agony. And besides all this, between us and you a great
chasm has been fixed, so that those who want to go from here to you cannot,
nor can anyone cross over from there to us."*

What we learn: Still the same parable. Abraham makes it clear
that there's a significant divide between heaven and hell. You can
talk across it, but traveling back-and-forth is not an option.

Questions/comments: The barrier probably exists, not so
much to keep heaven's residents out of hell but to keep the riff-raff
away from the milk and honey. Or, you know, the soothing drops of
water.

---

7. Kinda matches up with the two-sections-of-*Sheol* idea from the Book of Enoch,
does it not?

✹ 2 Thessalonians 1:8–9

He will punish those who do not know God and do not obey the gospel of our Lord Jesus. They will be punished with everlasting destruction and shut out from the presence of the Lord and from the majesty of his power.

What we learn: When Jesus comes back, the disobedient will be subject to everlasting destruction. Also? They'll be separated from God's presence and power.

Questions/comments: In case the everlasting destruction isn't bad enough.

✹ James 3:6

The tongue also is a fire, a world of evil among the parts of the body. It corrupts the whole person, sets the whole course of his life on fire, and is itself set on fire by hell.

Word used: *Gehenna*

What we learn: The tendency of humans to speak evil things has its origins in the fires of hell.

Questions/comments: Tongue on fire? Hopefully a figure of speech.

✹ 2 Peter 2:4

For if God did not spare angels when they sinned, but sent them to hell, putting them into gloomy dungeons to be held for judgment. . . .

Word used: *Tartaroo*

What we learn: This is the *Tartarus* verse, and it informs us that hell has dungeons. Gloomy dungeons. Which is sorta bad news. But the good news is that they seem to be reserved not for people but for fallen angels, who reside in them as holding cells prior to judgment.

> *"The only thing I could say for sure is that hell means separation from God. We are separated from his light, from his fellowship. That is going to be hell. When it comes to a literal fire, I don't preach it because I'm not sure about it. When the Scripture uses fire concerning hell, that is possibly an illustration of how terrible it's going to be—not fire but something worse, a thirst for God that cannot be quenched."*
>
> (Billy Graham in *Time,* November 15, 1993)

⚜ Jude 7

In a similar way, Sodom and Gomorrah and the surrounding towns gave themselves up to sexual immorality and perversion. They serve as an example of those who suffer the punishment of eternal fire.

What we learn: Wanna know what eternal punishment looks like? Check out the story of Sodom and Gomorrah. According to Genesis 19:24–25, it involved the raining down of "burning sulfur" upon every inhabitant of those cities, and the wholesale destruction of the landscape and vegetation around them.[8]

Questions/comments: Curiously, the punishment of Sodom and Gomorrah was a one-time act of annihilation—not a continuous rain of burning sulfur—so is it really the best example of punishment by "eternal fire"? Come on, Jude.

⚜ Revelation 1:18

I am the Living One; I was dead, and behold I am alive for ever and ever! And I hold the keys of death and Hades.

---

8. The King James Version of the Bible famously translates the *burning sulfur* phrase as "brimstone and fire."

Word used: *Hades*

What we learn: Jesus, having defeated death through the resurrection, holds the metaphorical keys to death and Hades. This indicates his control over them.

Questions/comments: Unless he *literally* holds the keys to hell, and in that case, why doesn't he lock the place up and, well, throw away the key?

✸ Revelation 6:8

I looked, and there before me was a pale horse! Its rider was named Death, and Hades was following close behind him. They were given power over a fourth of the earth to kill by sword, famine and plague, and by the wild beasts of the earth.

Word used: *Hades*

What we learn: Hell, when personified as Hades, rides a horse, is a sword–wielding assassin, spreads sickness, and can summon wild beasts to do his bidding. Like Aquaman but for nefarious purposes. And without the water.

Questions/comments: Or, on second thought, the passage may be speaking metaphorically. The Aquaman analogy is now off the table.

✸ Revelation 14:9–11

If anyone worships the beast and his image and receives his mark on the forehead or on the hand, he, too, will drink of the wine of God's fury, which has been poured full strength into the cup of his wrath. He will be tormented with burning sulfur in the presence of the holy angels and of the Lamb. And the smoke of their torment rises for ever and ever. There is no rest day or night for those who worship the beast and his image, or for anyone who receives the mark of his name.

171

What we learn: If you're on the wrong side of God during the last days, you'll be met with the Almighty's fury, which means a shower of burning sulfur in full sight of his throne. And it won't be a one-and-done thing: you'll smoke for ever and ever, with no rest.

Questions/comments: Yikes. Try not to worship the Antichrist. Don't let him stamp his mark on your forehead. And, while you're at it, treat any government-issued microchip implants with suspicion, too.

✹ Revelation 20:10

And the devil, who deceived them, was thrown into the lake of burning sulfur, where the beast and the false prophet had been thrown. They will be tormented day and night for ever and ever.

What we learn: Satan himself will eventually be subject to the fiery torture of hell—and yes, it appears to be perpetual—along with his minions.

Questions/comments: In a satisfying twist, the torturer becomes the torturee. But who takes over after that? Isn't he supposed to be running the place?

✹ Revelation 20:14

Then death and Hades were thrown into the lake of fire. The lake of fire is the second death.

Word used: *Hades*

What we learn: If Hades here is considered hell, a plain reading of this text seems to indicate that eventually hell itself will be destroyed, along with death.

Questions/comments: But that doesn't really jive with the "everlasting torment" stuff. Try to avoid a plain reading of the text.

✺ Revelation 20:15

If anyone's name was not found written in the book of life, he was thrown into the lake of fire.

What we learn: A fiery fate—like an eternal version of the Cuyahoga River[9]—awaits those who don't make the list. And Satan's in there, too, so watch out.

Questions/comments: It's probably a really long list, so if your name doesn't appear, try your maiden name. Or nicknames. Whatever you do, make sure the bookkeeper double-checks that thing.

✺ Revelation 21:8

But the cowardly, the unbelieving, the vile, the murderers, the sexually immoral, those who practice magic arts, the idolaters and all liars—their place will be in the fiery lake of burning sulfur. This is the second death.

What we learn: If you're a coward, unbeliever, evil person, murderer, fornicator, sorcerer, magic enthusiast, idolater, or liar, you'd better watch out. Or invent an eternally guaranteed firesuit.

Questions/comments: The "magic arts" thing seems out of place, though being in hell with Lance Burton, or David Blaine, or David Copperfield—or pretty much any magician—*does* seem like a special kind of torture.

---

9. An Ohio river known for having once been so polluted with oil and debris that it occasionally caught fire.

CHAPTER 7

The Afterlists
(Cataloging Kingdom Come)

According to many traditions and cultures, the afterlife goes on and on and on. Eternally. Perpetually. Everlastingly. But books about the afterlife—especially the small ones—have to end. And what better way to end than with a brief collection of random lists?

The subject lends itself, after all, to listy-ness. There are all those chambers of hell in Chinese mythology. And those hellish punishments so brilliantly described by Dante. And the synonyms and symbols and signs and sightings just begging to be assigned categories and numbers.

So here they are. May the time you spend in these pages be accompanied by more bliss than torment.

Seven Hard-to-Pronounce Proper Names Appearing in This Book and Their Phonetic Pronunciations

1. *Hades* (hay-DEEZ): The underworld of Greek mythology. It rhymes with "ladies." It does not rhyme with "spades." Dork.

2. *Yggdrasil* (igg-DRAH-sil): The monumental ash tree at the center of the Old Norse universe, with Asgard in its branches and Niflheim beneath its roots.

3. *Zaqqum* (zuh-KOOM): A tree growing in Jahannah, the Muslim hell. It produces gut-busting devil-headed fruit.

4. *Phlegython* (fleg-ih-THAHN): A flaming river in Hades that empties into the torturous realm of Tartarus.

5. *Maat* (muh-AHT): The ancient Egyptian goddess of truth and justice, whose feather is weighed against your heart to determine whether you go to paradise or, you know, get eaten by a demon.

6. *Mictlantecuhtli* (mik-tlan-tuh-COO-tli): The Aztec god of death. He's usually depicted as a skeleton dripping with blood, which is almost scarier than having to pronounce his name.

7. *Mictecacihuatl* (mik-tuh-cac-i-KWA-tl): The wife of Mictlantecuhtli. The *Pocket Guide* assumes these two deathly lovers had simpler nicknames for each other. Because freedom from tongue-twisters is important to rulers of the underworld.

Six Things You Didn't Know About Death, If by "Death" You Mean Thanatos, the Personification of Death in Ancient Greek Mythology

1. Death is only a minor deity.

2. Death's parents are Erebos (Darkness) and Nyx (Night).

3. Death has a twin brother, Hypnos (Sleep).

4. Death has other siblings, including Geras (Old Age), Moros (Doom), and Oizys (Suffering).

5. Death and his brothers and sisters are no doubt real rays of sunshine in their neighborhood.

6. Death totally got schooled once by Hercules in a fight.

Seven Random Names and Descriptions of the Death Deity in Various Cultures

1. *Ah Puch,* the bell-wearing, owl-headed, skeleton-bodied god of death (Mayan mythology).

2. *Giltine,* a formerly pretty young thing who was trapped in a coffin for seven years and emerged as a horrible old woman with a long blue nose and freaky-lickin' poisonous tongue (Lithuanian paganism).

3. *The Grim Reaper,* a black-hooded, gown-wearing, skeletal creep with a scythe (Western/English pop mythology).

4. *Izanami,* the maggot-infested goddess of death who takes a thousand lives a day (Japanese mythology).

5. *Joe Black,* the scruffily handsome character played by Brad Pitt in the 1998 film remake *Meet Joe Black* (American cinema).

6. *Marzanna,* an old woman in white clothes, carrying a green sprout (Slavic paganism).

7. *Yama,* the green-skinned Lord of death who rides a water buffalo (Hindu mythology).

Eighteen Symbols of Death Throughout the Ages

1. Skull
2. Skeleton
3. Hooded Grim Reaper
4. River
5. Boat
6. Bridge
7. Candle
8. Hourglass
9. Pearly Gates
10. Wreath
11. Gravestone
12. Crows
13. Bats
14. Vultures
15. Black Cats
16. Cross
17. Wheel
18. Keith Richards

Six General Afterlife-Related Beliefs of African Ancestor Cults

1. *Ancestors are powerful.* Certain high-ranking people in the living realm—like kings, chiefs, and elders—become powerful ancestors who continue to influence the tribe after they die, and are consulted on almost every aspect of life in the community.

2. *Some ancestors are less powerful.* Regular nonruling dead people are honored for a while after they die, but their influence is minimal, and eventually they are forgotten.

3. *Ancestors communicate in different ways.* When questioned by the village, an ancestor may—in ascending order of freakiness— hide his answers in dreams, reveal them through divination, or possess the body of a villager and speak audibly through him or her.

4. *It pays to keep ancestors happy.* Happy ancestors can be relied upon to provide a healthy birth, or favorable weather, or fertile soil. Unhappy ancestors? They're responsible for tribal misfortune, famine, sickness, personal injury, and death. If gramps wakes up on the wrong side of the coffin? Watch out.

5. *Ancestors can hang out anywhere.* They may be floating in and around their grave, or attached to a favorite possession, or sharing a room with their closest relative. Or they may be doing time in some vague Ancestorland underground or in the sky.

6. *Morality or virtue make no difference when it comes to the afterlife.* Your social standing is a very big deal in the world of ancestor cults. But your behavior? Completely irrelevant. So tribal Africa is a lot like Washington, D.C.

Eight Specific Afterlife-Related Beliefs of African Ancestor Cults

1. When a spirit becomes an ancestor, he "crosses the water" to a shiny, new, clean underground village where he takes up a life

not too different from the one he just left. This happens for ten cycles of birth, death, and ancestor inauguration. *(Mende people, Sierra Leone)*

2. Upon the experience of misfortune, it often helps to make a sacrifice at the grave of an ancestor—even if you've already converted to Christianity or Islam. *(Luguru people, Tanzania)*

3. Wanna become a quality ancestor? A male offspring is an important requirement. You can be the wisest, most virtuous man in the village, but if you have no surviving sons, no ancestor-dom for you. *(Tallensi people, Ghana)*

4. Each person has a fixed lifespan and purpose, and may be reincarnated if he or she has been a good boy or girl. Bad people, however, get punished. *(Yoruba people, Nigeria)*

5. In order for a dead person to reach the land of his ancestors, he must pay a ferryman and cross a river. Which isn't a big deal, unless the person died owing someone money. If that's the case, he has to wait until his creditor shows up with payment. It's even worse for bad people, who don't even get to use the ferry. They have to swim across the river. This takes three years. Apparently, it's a wide river. *(LoDagaa people, Ghana)*

6. Some people get buried twice. First right after death, in a big grave stocked with its own bed. The deceased is arranged so his eyes face the land of the tribe's origin. The next burial happens several months later, after a period of mourning has finished. In burial #2, an elder strikes the grave with a switch from a special tree. The deceased's spirit enters the switch, which is then taken to the home of the dead person and transferred into an object

the community will find worthwhile. Like an ax. Or a hoe. Or a coin. Which means you'd better have a real good reason to spend Uncle Mboko's quarter. *(Yombe people, Zambia)*

7. The spirit leaves the body after death but still hovers around the family, and even shares meals with them. So families set small portions of food aside for their dead ancestors' hovering spirits. *(Basotho people, South Africa and Lesotho)*

8. When a person dies, all relatives are expected, if at all possible, to attend the funeral to pay their respects. Therefore all relatives must be informed of a family death—even the ones who live really far away. If modern conveniences like cell phones are unavailable for this purpose, there's still no excuse for not showing up. Because they should have been made aware of the death via magic. Obviously. *(Bantu-speaking people, sub-Saharan Africa)*

Eleven Highly Attractive Synonyms for Heaven

1. Paradise
2. Eternal Bliss
3. Eternal Rest
4. Promised Land
5. The Sweet By-and-By
6. Life Everlasting
7. Happy Hunting Ground
8. Nirvana
9. The Blessed State
10. The Blue
11. Dreamland

One Profoundly Unattractive Synonym for Heaven

1. The Bosom of Abraham

One Generally Neutral Synonym for Heaven

1. The Great Unknown

The Five Chambers of the Jewish Heaven (Gan Eden) as Described in the Midrash *Konen*

1. The cedar chamber with a roof of transparent crystal, occupied by non-Jews who convert to the faith. Here, the prophet Obadiah teaches them the Law.

2. The cedar chamber with a ceiling of silver, occupied by penitents. Here, Manasseh, the king of Israel, teaches them the Law.

3. The really huge chamber of silver and gold and pearl ornamentation, occupied by all the patriarchs and tribes of Israel and those who perished during the Exodus. Pretty much all generations of Israel are here. Moses teaches them the law in this realm. The Tree of Life is in the center of this chamber, and the chamber's entrance is guarded against living mortals by a giant glowing sword.

4. The chamber of olive wood, occupied by those who suffered for their faith.

5. The chamber of precious stones, gold, and silver on the banks of the legendary river Gihon. Here is where Elijah and the Messiah dwell.

Six Hard-to-Describe Revelations About Heaven, as Described by Don Piper in *90 Minutes in Heaven*

1. It is really hard to write about the experience, on account of how earthly terms fail to do it justice.

2. Heaven feels like you are in another dimension. No, really, *it does!*

3. The streets of heaven really are paved of gold. Literal gold. Like a regular brick street . . . only the bricks are solid gold! But it's so amazing that the use of a word like *gold* is insufficient.

4. The Pearly Gates aren't really pearly, but pearlescent. Or maybe iridescent. Or shimmery. Sigh. You kind of had to be there.

5. The music of heaven is filled with classic hymns and modern worship songs, but no sad songs. It's all happy praise music in heaven. Inexpressibly happy.

6. For the above reason, there are no songs in heaven about Jesus dying on the cross, which was a sad event, even though the eventual outcome was happy. It's complicated. Honestly, it's too complicated to explain. Like heaven.

Eight Surprises About Hell, as Described by Bill Wiese in *23 Minutes in Hell*

1. Hell really is located underground, beneath the surface of the earth.

2. Demons smell like the sum of all the rottenest things in the world, multiplied a thousand times. Mathematically, Wiese's description looks like this: *Demon stench = (open sewer + rotten meat + spoiled eggs + sour milk + dead rotting animal flesh + sulfur) x 1,000.*

3. Lots of other things in hell are multiplied by 1,000, including the strength of demons, the loudness of screams, the dryness of the air, and the net worth of a book-writin' California real estate agent.

4. There are no blades of grass or green leaves in hell.

5. There are demons who look like disfigured bears and grotesque gorillas. Some have long arms. Others have large feet. Most of them are chained to the cave-like walls of hell.

6. The really massive weightlifter guy Bill Wiese and his wife used to see at the gym would be no match for these demons in a fight.

7. There are giant rats and spiders in hell. And snakes and worms of various sizes.

8. Hell is full of small pits, three to five feet across and four to five feet deep, "each holding a single lost soul."[1]

---

1. Wiese, B. *23 Minutes in Hell* (Lake Mary, FL: Charisma House, 2006), p. 30.

Ten Torments Observed in the Eighth Circle of Hell, According to Dante's *Inferno*[2]

1. Being whipped by horned demons with "great scourges," who force seducers and panderers to march forever and ever, back and forth, back and forth, back and forth . . . (Canto XVIII).

2. Being smothered in poo—also known as that which floweth out of "human privies"—due to too much flattery during life (Canto XVIII).

3. Being placed head-first and upside-down into a hole in a rock, with legs sticking out and feet on fire, as a punishment for simony (Canto XIX).[3]

4. Having one's head violently rotated 180 degrees, from front to back, to force fortune-tellers to look the wrong direction all the time—made even more difficult due to their constant weeping (Canto XX).

5. Being immersed in cauldrons of boiling oil by "black devils" who have hooks and rakes to keep crooked politicians in place (Canto XXI).

6. Being forced to trudge around aimlessly while wearing an "everlastingly fatiguing" hooded cloak that's all shiny and

---

2. All quotes taken from Henry Wadsworth Longfellow's English translation of Dante's original work in Italian (available online at www.divinecomedy.org).

3. *Simony* is the use of money to purchase or sell things of spiritual value, like buying and selling pardons or ecclesiastical offices or spiritual blessings. It's named after the magician Simon Magus, who in Acts 8 tries to offer cash to Christ's disciples in exchange for them giving him the power of the Holy Spirit. Because, oh, the tricks he could do!

gold-covered but also made of lead and therefore super-heavy. This is a punishment for being a hypocrite (Canto XXIII).

7. Being chased around naked by a "terrible throng of serpents" with no means of escape, as a punishment for being a thief. Even worse, once bitten, the thief flames up, burns to a crisp, disintegrates into a pile of ash, then gets reassembled so the horror can start all over again (Canto XXIV).[4]

8. Being enclosed—as an "evil counselor"—in one's own personal everlasting flame. Don't give bad advice (Canto XXVI).

9. Being poked, sliced, shredded, dismembered, and otherwise mutilated by demons who use hellish swords to hack off the arms and open up the guts and stab through the necks of "disseminators of scandal and of schism." Then the wounds heal up. Then the demons go at it again (Canto XXVIII).

10. Being afflicted with eternal leprosy and other flesh-destroying diseases that come from a sickening moat, which emits a stench "as from putrescent limbs is wont to issue," as punishment for being a counterfeiter, evil impersonator, and/or other kind of "falsifier" (Cantos XXIX and XXX).

Nine Surprising Things Revealed About Satan in Dante's *Inferno*

1. He doesn't rule the entirety of hell but instead dwells in its lowest, most centralized level.

---

4. That's not the only result of being bitten. Other victims morph into horrifying lizard-y creatures, or swap souls with the snakes and end up biting their fellow thieves. Dante's a genius.

2. He's not burning with fire and brimstone or walking around in red leotard, but instead is frozen, from the waist down, in a block of ice.

3. He has three sets of bat-like wings and keeps flapping them around in an attempt to escape. But the breeze only serves to keep the ice properly chilled.

4. He has three faces. One is red. The other two are black and pale yellow.

5. Each face has two eyes. All six eyes are crying.

6. Each face has a mouth. Each mouth perpetually chews on a person known for having been a traitor.

7. The two outside mouths gnaw on Cassius and Brutus of Caesar-assassinating fame.

8. The middle mouth, with the sharpest teeth, crunches Judas Iscariot, the betrayer of Jesus Christ. Judas' head never escapes the devil's mouth, but that's not even the worst part. While he's crunching the Bad Disciple's head, Satan uses his claws to continually strip skin off Judas' back so that his spine remains exposed.

9. Pitchforks, cloven hooves, and/or pointy tails do not make an appearance.

The Seven Deadly Sins and Ways People Might Be Purified from Them in Purgatory, According to Dante's *Purgatorio*

1. *Pride:* By trudging around while toting huge stones on their backs, which bend them to the ground and keep their eyes downcast (Cantos X to XII).

2. *Envy:* By having their eyelids sewn shut by an iron wire, which "presses out [their] tears so that they bathed their cheeks," and wearing clothes that cause them to blend in with their surroundings (Cantos XIII to XV).

3. *Wrath:* By stumbling around in a "bitter and foul air" that obscures their eyesight with a smoky haze. Because the blinding smoke is a clever metaphor for blinding rage (Cantos XV to XVII).

4. *Sloth:* By running around Purgatory in a big group, while showing "an eager fervour." A lot like the start of a marathon, but with more weeping (Cantos XVII and XIX).

5. *Greed:* By lying face-down and paralyzed on the ground while sighing and moaning incoherently (Cantos XIX to XXI).

6. *Gluttony:* By being forced into "emaciation and sad squalor" by being placed in the presence of sweet-smelling apples and fountains of delicious water, and yet remaining unable to partake of them (Cantos XXII to XXIV).

7. *Lust:* By compelling "the wanton" to walk repeatedly through an embankment of intense flame, until it sears the hoochie wanton sexiness right out of them (Cantos XXV to XXVII).

Seven Methods of Torture Observed in Hell by Moses, as Revealed in a Jewish Midrash Legend Called *The Revelation of Moses*

1. Being suspended by your eyelids, because you lusted after married women, or money, or property.[5]

2. Being suspended by your tongue, for slandering your neighbor and speaking vain and empty words.

3. Being suspended by your ears, for having neglected the study of the law.

4. Being suspended by your hands, for using them to steal and murder.

5. Being suspended by your hair and breasts (women only), for having employed those parts to tempt men into lust.

6. Being suspended by your, um, manhood (men only), for having used it to commit adultery.

---

5. For what it's worth, all suspensions are by "chains of fire."

7. Being suspended by your feet and being covered with long black worms, for having lied, profaned the Sabbath, persecuted orphans, and called your neighbor bad names.

Twenty-Four Segments of Hell in Hindu Mythology and Their Plainly Descriptive English Meanings[6]

1. *Raurava* (Horrifying)

2. *Maharaurava* (Most Horrifying)

3. *Tamisra* (Dark)

4. *Andhatamisraka* (Utter Dark)

5. *Kalacakra* (Wheel of Time)

6. *Apratistha* (Foundationless)

7. *Ghatiyantra* (Diarrhea)

8. *Asipatravana* (Forest of Sword Blades)

9. *Taptakumbha* (Burning Vat)

10. *Kutasalmali* (Thorny)

11. *Karapatra* (Saw-Toothed)

12. *Svanabhojana* (Dog-Eating)

13. *Samdamsa* (Pincers)

14. *Lohapinda* (Red Hot Iron Balls)[7]

---

6. These come from the Vamana Purana, a Hindu religious text dating from 300–1000 C.E. From *Classical Hindu Mythology: A Reader in the Sanskrit Puranas,* C. Dimmitt, ed., and J.A.B. van Buitenen, trans. (Philadelphia: Temple University Press, 1978), pp. 49–50.
7. This may or may not also be the title of an adult film.

15. *Karambhasikata* (Groat-Gravel)

16. *Ghora* (Horrible)

17. *Ksaranadi* (Ash-River)

18. *Krmibhojana* (Worm-Eating)

19. *Sonitapuyabhojana* (Blood- and Pus-Eating)

20. *Nisita* (Sharp)

21. *Ksuragradharo* (Razor-Edge Sharp)

22. *Cakraka* (Wheel)

23. *Samsosana* (Drying Up)

24. *Ananta* (Endless)

Eighteen Chambers in the Tenth Court of Diyu, the Hell of Chinese Mythology, and the Terrible Things That Occur Within Them

1. *Chamber of Wind and Thunder:* Where murderers and really greedy perpetrators are punished, presumably by getting their hair blown out of place and by having to listen to loud, percussive sounds.

2. *Chamber of Grinding:* Where food-wasting, unproductive rich dudes get ground up into powder.[8]

3. *Chamber of Flames:* Where thieves, robbers, and other cheaters get the fiery treatment.

---

8. Lesson #1 of Chinese Mythology: It's better to be a murderer than a wealthy lush. The *Pocket Guide* would totally prefer "wind and thunder" to live pulverization in the afterlife.

191

4. *Chamber of Ice:* Where kids who treat their parents poorly are frozen in ice, which is kinda rough considering that's the same punishment Satan gets (see p. 187).

5. *Chamber of Oil Cauldrons:* Where adulterers, rapists, and other sexual deviants are fried up in vats of oil, extra crispy.

6. *Chamber of Dismemberment by Sawing:* Where kidnappers who force women into prostitution end up participating in that old sawed-in-half magic trick, only it's not magic.

7. *Chamber of Dismemberment by Chariot:* Where corrupt government officials and/or exploitative landlords get crushed, sliced, and otherwise broken into small pieces. By a chariot. Obviously.

8. *Chamber of Mountain of Knives:* Where unethical merchants and/or unscrupulous shopkeepers bleed to death because they're forced to go all Edmund Hillary on a really sharp, pointy mountain.

9. *Chamber of Tongue Ripping:* Where troublemaking gossips and liars have their tongues ripped out.

10. *Chamber of Pounding:* Where cold-blooded murderers—presumably worse than the ones listed in #1—are beaten into a pulpy sludge.

11. *Chamber of Torso-Severing:* Where schemers and unappreciative underlings lose their stomachs in pretty much the most literal way possible.

12. *Chamber of Scales:* Where disrespectful daughters-in-law and those who oppress the innocent get hooks jammed into their bodies, and then are hung upside down for an indefinite time.

13. *Chamber of Eye-Gouging:* Where pervs, peeping toms, and other leering weirdos get their eyeballs poked out in a violent fashion.

14. *Chamber of Heart-Digging:* Where those with darkness and evil in their hearts get those same nasty hearts scooped out of their chest.

15. *Chamber of Disembowelment:* Where tomb raiders get bowel-raided. Same goes for hypocrites.

16. *Chamber of Blood:* Where blasphemers and others who disrespect the gods get flayed alive. Presumably it involves a modest amount of blood.

17. *Chamber of Maggots:* Where those who scheme and tiptoe around the law for personal gain get consumed—very slowly—by a whole squirming mess of maggots.

18. *Chamber of Avici:* You thought the first 17 chambers were bad? This one's worse. It's for the super-evil, including those who kill their parents or betray the king. They are placed on a tiny platform over a raging inferno. If they fall off, they burn up and are then reborn—right back on the platform. Which means no reincarnation. Which also means this is the one chamber of hell that's not temporary. It's pretty much eternal.

Six Helpful Spells Listed in the *Papyrus of Ani*, the Egyptian *Book of the Dead* from Around 1250 B.C.

1. A spell for not letting the heart-case of a man be taken away from him in the underworld (chapter 29)

2. A spell for not letting the head of a man be cut off from his body in the underworld (chapter 43)

3. A spell for not dying a second time in the underworld (chapter 44)

4. A spell for not rotting in the underworld (chapter 45)

5. A spell for snuffing the air, and of having power over the water in the underworld (chapter 58)

6. A spell for not being transported to the East in the underworld (chapter 93)[9]

Twelve Activities That May Be Signs of an Impending Death Should They Occur in Your Dreams, According to the Tibetan *Book of the Dead*

1. Being disemboweled by a fierce black woman, causing your entrails to spill out

2. Eating feces

3. Wearing black clothes of yak hair

4. Being trapped in a wicker basket

5. Being dragged by a black rope attached to the neck

6. Being trapped inside a very tall, red-colored, moat-surrounded castle

7. Being decapitated and having your head carried away by someone else

---

9. All based on *The Papyrus of Ani* (The Egyptian *Book of the Dead*), translated by E. A. Wallis Budge (accessed at http://eawc.evansville.edu/anthology/ani.htm).

8. Repeatedly picking red flowers

9. Being dragged along by a crowd of dead people

10. Being surrounded by crows, or villains

11. Dancing with a host of ogres

12. Jumping headlong into a pit

Sixteen Famous Ghosts (or Combinations of Ghosts)

1. Beetlejuice

2. The Bell Witch[10]

3. Blinky, Pinky, Inky, Clyde (nemeses of Pac-Man)

4. Bloody Mary

5. Caspar (the friendly ghost)

6. Hamlet's Father

7. The Headless Horseman of Sleepy Hollow

8. The Holy Ghost

9. La Llorona[11]

---

10. The legendary ghost from a series of alleged nineteenth-century hauntings in Tennessee. Apparently, the ghost had feminine characteristics. So she must have been a witch. This was good news for modern indie cinema, because the Bell Witch legend inspired *The Blair Witch Project*. The Blair Ghost Project isn't nearly as cool a movie name.

11. A spooky lady in Hispanic folklore who walks the banks of rivers and lakes weeping for her dead children. Also: They're dead because she drowned them. If you see her, watch out, because she may attempt to drown you, too.

10. The Lorelei[12]

11. Jacob Marley

12. The Ghosts of Christmas Past, Present, and Future

13. The Stay-Puft Marshmallow Man

14. The Vanishing Hitchhiker

15. Patrick Swayze

16. (Spoiler Alert!) Bruce Willis

Eight Famous Ghostly Locations

1. *Drury Lane* (Theatre Royale, Drury Lane, London): The most haunted theater in England and alleged home to several ghosts. The most famous of these spirit squatters is the "Man in Grey," an eighteenth-century nobleman in a gray riding coat whose skeleton, according to legend, was once discovered with a knife sticking out of his ribs. Other ghosts, including those of eighteenth-century performers Charles Macklin and Joe Grimaldi, are also said to show up backstage, from time to time.

2. *Raynham Hall* (Norfolk, England): Home of the "Brown Lady," the subject of the most famous ghost photograph in history. Though the Brown Lady hasn't been seen since her staircase-descending portrait was taken in 1936, she appeared several times prior to that coming-out party. She's said to wear a

---

12. A maiden in German folklore who killed herself by leaping from a huge rock on the Rhine River. Because an unfaithful lover caused her to do the deed, she gets back at all men by luring sailors to their death with her echoing, siren-like voice.

brown satin dress (pretty!) and have empty black holes for eye sockets (not so pretty!). The famous photograph wasn't planned; a camera crew was on hand at Raynham Hall for a magazine shoot when everyone was suddenly all, "Look! The Brown Lady! If only we had a camera! *(pause)* Aha!"

3. *The Borley Rectory* (Borley, Essex, England): Known as the most haunted house in England, the Borley Rectory is said to be home to multiple ghosts and/or poltergeists. One may have been a thirteenth-century nun who fell in love with a monk, tried to elope, but was captured and bricked up in the rectory's walls. The other may have been the Rev. Harry Bull, who supposedly passed away at Borley yet continues to walk its halls in a gray jacket he'd been wearing at the time of death. The rectory came to prominence when the popular 1930s ghost hunter Harry Price investigated it and reported on the ghostly phenomena he experienced—which included mysterious tappings, unexplained footsteps, ringing bells, writing on walls, and people being thrown out of bed—before the place burned down in 1937.

4. *The Chase Vault* (Christ Church, Barbados): In the ancient Christ Church cemetery on the island of Barbados is a mausoleum known as the Chase Vault. In 1807, a woman named Mrs. Goddard was buried in the vault. The next year, it was purchased by the Chase family, who used it to bury an infant daughter in 1808 and another daughter in 1812. Both were interred in heavy, lead-lined caskets, and the vault was sealed with a marble slab. The family's patriarch, Thomas Chase, also died in 1812. But when the family broke the seal to insert Papa's casket, they discovered the other caskets had clearly

been messed with. One stood on end, upside-down. *Thieves! Vandals! Outrage!* The next time it was opened, four years later, the caskets had been messed with again—even though Thomas Chase's casket was so heavy it had taken eight men to put it in place the first time. *Um . . . surprisingly strong vandals!* Two more times over the next few years the vault was opened, and both times the caskets were found to be in severe disarray. The authorities were stunned. They looked for secret entrances or any other clues. Nothing. So they scattered sand on the floor to record footprints before cementing it up again. In 1820, the seal was broken one last time to inter a body—and, yep, caskets all over the place. The sand was undisturbed. By this time, the cemetery authorities had developed a good case of the shivers, so they abandoned the vault and put the coffins somewhere else. The mystery has never been solved.

5. *112 Ocean Avenue, Amityville, New York* (Long Island): In 1974, Ronald DeFeo Jr. shot his mother, father, two sisters, and two brothers to death in a house on Ocean Avenue. Thirteen months later, the Lutz family moved in. Twenty-eight days later, the Lutzes moved out. In a hurry. Why? Because of the swarms of flies, phantom cold spots, phantom excrement smells, phantom door-slamming, phantom marching band noises, green slime oozing from walls, levitating family members, and a revolving crucifix on the wall, Not to mention their five-year-old daughter's new imaginary friend: a flying pig with red eyes. Scary things afoot in Amityville. One might describe it as a *horror,* in fact. But three decades and many films later, most investigators now believe the Lutz family just made the whole thing up. First clue? Flying pigs have *brown* eyes. Duh.

6. *Bachelor's Grove Cemetery* (near Chicago): This abandoned cemetery between Midlothian and Oak Grove near Chicago has long been considered one of the most haunted places in America—thanks to frequent vandalism (which makes it seem dangerous), its dark forest setting (which makes it spookier), and a bunch of paranormal reports that peaked once it turned into a great make-out place for teens in the 1970s (fear leads to cuddling). Ghost sightings include glowing orbs, a phantom farmhouse with a squeaky porch swing, and a shimmery woman in white who was once photographed sitting on a tombstone.

7. *The St. James Hotel* (Cimarron, New Mexico): This inn and saloon on the Santa Fe Trail once hosted Old West luminaries like Kit Carson, Billy the Kid, Wyatt Earp, and Jesse James. And apparently, it's still hosting a few of their old dead friends. Still in operation, the hotel receives guests year-round in its historic rooms—except for Room 18, which remains locked and is allegedly home to the angry spirit of a poker player who was shot in its doorway, only to drag himself into the room, where he died. Also roaming its halls are the original owner's second wife (who smells like roses); a dwarf-like old man hotel staffers call "the Little Imp" (who steals things); and random cowboy ghosts who stop by every once in awhile to play random hands of poker (seriously).

8. *The World's Oceans:* Home to the *Flying Dutchman,* history's famed ghost ship. According to legend, the *Flying Dutchman* was headed to Holland in 1641. As it rounded the Cape of Good Hope, a huge storm blew up but the captain refused to back down. He cursed God, swearing he'd never retreat from—*aaargh!*—something so sissy-like as a storm. Then he took it further, shaking his fist at the heavens and declaring that nothing could stop him from getting home. So God decided to, well, stop him from ever getting home. Just to show him who was Boss. Since that fateful day, sailors have reported seeing a glowing, phantom ship in various waters around the world. It was last sighted in 2006, in the second film in the *Pirates of the Caribbean* franchise, under the control of an octopus-faced ghost captain.

Twelve Possible Explanations for Ghosts

1. They are souls of the dead who have returned to finish an unfinished task.

2. They have returned to avenge their deaths.

3. They want to uncover a hidden truth.

4. They are trying to protect their families.

5. They are suicide victims bound to wander the earth aimlessly.

6. They did not receive the proper burial rites.

7. They are ancestors looking out for us.

8. They are somehow trapped in this dimension and trying to find a way out.

9. They are projections of your subconscious.

10. They are hallucinations.

11. They are only floating bedsheets with eyeholes and nothing to be afraid of.

12. They are at Stage Three of the four stages of death prior to the next resurrection, with Stage One being an animal and Stage Two being a demon (Burmese Buddhism only).

One Heebie-Jeebie-Inducing Explanation for Ghosts

1. They are cruel spirits intent on stealing children (African folklore only).

Eight Things That Typically Occur During a Near-Death Experience, According to Raymond A. Moody's *Life After Life*

1. *You hear a buzzing or ringing noise.* This should tip you off that you're dead. It can be a confusing realization to make, but just roll with it.

2. *Your pain disappears.* The pain of death and sickness? Gone. What you're left with is peace and pain relief. This is quite refreshing.

3. *You get a bit floaty.* You might have the sensation of rising out of your own body and hovering above it. This is called an out-of-body experience. Sure, it's kinda weird to watch the doctors and nurses poking around your bloody, cracked-open body cavity, but ultimately the experience is a lot more serene than you'd expect.

4. *You enter the "dark tunnel."* You travel through that tunnel at high speed. At the end of the tunnel is a light. Depending on the condition of your earthly existence at the time of near-death, you're either going to want to race toward the light or avoid it at all costs. You make the call.

5. *You encounter "people of light."* Don't freak out: they're nice. In fact, you probably know them. Most likely it's a welcoming party attended by all the friends and family who preceded you in death. They'll look pretty much the same as they used to, only a lot brighter. Try not to squint, though. It's rude.

6. *You encounter a "being of light."* This is no normal friend or relative. It's a powerful spiritual entity, like God, or Jesus, or an angel, or Oprah. Contrary to popular belief, this person won't make you feel guilty, but will instead make you feel good about yourself. Self-esteem is important to beings of light.

7. *You experience the dreaded "life review."* Your life flashes before your eyes as you visually relive all your good and bad deeds. The effect of this is like a heavenly slideshow, and is supposedly pretty cool. Especially if you've performed more good than bad deeds.

8. *You get sent away and this bums you out.* The being of light may tell you it's not yet your time. Don't be concerned, though, if Jesus starts shoving you back into the tunnel. It's not because he and Oprah don't love you. It's so you can return to your loved ones, back among the living. Either way, you know leaving is the right thing to do but can't shake the feeling that you're missing out on something seriously good.[13]

---

13. From the second chapter ("The Experience of Dying") in Moody, R., and Kübler-Ross, E. *Life After Life: The Investigation of a Phenomenon—Survival of Bodily Death* (New York: HarperCollins, 2001. Originally published in 1975.)

One Brutally Ironic Book to Have Completed Shortly Before You Expired

1. *Survival After Death,* an unpublished manuscript written by Duke sociologist and psychical researcher Hornell Norris Hart. He died in 1967 before he could get it published.

SELECTED BIBLIOGRAPHY

The following titles are much more scholarly than this book and therefore were of eternal significance in assembling the *Pocket Guide*. Should you take offense at any errors, omissions, misspellings, and/or annoyances in the preceding pages, it is not the fault of the books or authors below. It is most likely the *Pocket Guide*'s fault. Or, perhaps, your time on earth has ended and this is the first stage of a literary purgatory designed to cleanse your soul from being so nit-picky about things like that. In that case, welcome. And good luck.

Blum, D. *Ghost Hunters: William James and the Search for Scientific Proof of Life After Death* (New York: Penguin, 2006).

Bonnefoy, Y., Doniger, W., and Honigsblum, G. *American, African, and Old European Mythologies* (Chicago: University of Chicago Press, 1993).

Bowker, J. *Oxford Concise Dictionary of World Religions* (Oxford: Oxford University Press, 2000).

Hamilton, E. *Mythology* (New York: Mentor, 1969).

Hathaway, N. *The Friendly Guide to Mythology* (New York: Viking, 2001).

SELECTED BIBLIOGRAPHY

Lewis, J. R. *Encyclopedia of Afterlife Beliefs and Phenomena* (Detroit: Visible Ink Press, 1995).

McDannel, C., and Lang, B. *Heaven: A History* (New Haven, CT: Yale University Press, 2001).

McGrath, A. E. *A Brief History of Heaven* (Malden, MA: Blackwell Publishing, Ltd., 2003).

Obayashi, H., ed. *Death and Afterlife: Perspectives of World Religions* (Westport, CT: Praeger Publishing, 1992).

Segal, A. F. *Life After Death: A History of the Afterlife in Western Religion* (New York: Doubleday, 2004).

Turner, A. K. *The History of Hell* (Orlando: Harcourt Brace, 1993).

The following two books are not considered "scholarly" at all. (In fact, a substantial number of people don't even consider them "true.") But they were invaluable inspirations for the writing of this book, and you should totally read them right now.

Piper, D., with Murphy, C. *90 Minutes in Heaven: A True Story of Death and Life* (Grand Rapids, MI: Revell, 2004).

Wiese, B. *23 Minutes in Hell* (Lake Mary, FL: Charisma House, 2006).

THE AUTHOR

Jason Boyett is the author of several books, including *Pocket Guide to the Bible*, *Pocket Guide to Sainthood*, and *Pocket Guide to the Apocalypse*. Though not a professional theologian or historian, he has long been fascinated by religion and history. And pockets, apparently. Which explains this series.

Jason has been featured on the History Channel and National Geographic Channel and also enjoys addressing audiences larger than a camera lens. He blogs regularly at www.jasonboyett.com, makes a lot of noise on Twitter (twitter.com/jasonboyett), and writes for a variety of publications. Jason lives in Texas with his wife, Aimee, and their two children.

Learn more about the *Pocket Guides* at www.pocketguidesite.com.

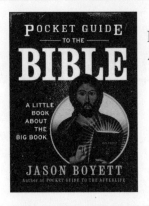

Pocket Guide to the Bible
A Little Book About the Big Book

Jason Boyett

Paperback | 208 pp.

ISBN: 978-0-4703-7309-5

This short, humorous guide to the Bible touches on the interesting, the touching, the off-beat, the unexpected, the unusual, and the downright weird. Including:

- ❖ Biblicabulary (A Glossary of the Good Book)
- ❖ Cast of Characters (A to Z)
- ❖ What Happens, Part 1 (The Old Testament at Breakneck Speed)
- ❖ What Happens, Part 2 (The New Testament at Breakneck Speed)
- ❖ The Brief History of Holy Writ (A Timeline)
- ❖ Versions and Perversions (A Selective Survey of Translations)
- ❖ List Ye Be Smitten (Biblical Flotsam and Jetsam)

Also by Jason Boyett

Pocket Guide to Sainthood
The Field Manual for the Super-Virtuous Life

Jason Boyett

Paperback | 224 pp.

ISBN: 978-0-4703-7310-1

This short, humorous guide to saints across the ages—the interesting, the touching, the off-beat, the unexpected, the unusual, and the downright weird. Including:

- ❖ There Should Have Been a St. Webster (A Glossary of Terms)
- ❖ Saints You Should Know (A-Z)
- ❖ There's a Saint for That (Patron Saints and Their Causes)
- ❖ The Canonization Process (in 18 Simple Steps)
- ❖ Sts. Flotsam and Jetsam (An Assortment of Lists)

Available Soon

The Boundary-Breaking God

An Unfolding Story of Hope and Promise

Danielle Shroyer

Hardcover | 144 pp.

ISBN: 978-0-4704-5100-7

The Boundary-Breaking God seeks to tell the story of God not as a one of preservation, but of exploration and expansion, a God who delights in breaking through boundaries, relishes popping up in unexpected places, and favors the outsider over the institutional insider.

Seeing God's story as a story of boundary breaking will open your imagination and encourage you to live as a person of hopeful purpose who attempts to change the world for the better. Rather than compartmentalizing faith to a "spiritualized" realm, faith in the boundary-breaking God engages life at every corner—social, economical, political, intellectual, ecological— and informs the way we faithfully respond in an increasingly complex world.

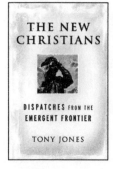

The New Christians
Dispatches from the Emergent Frontier
Tony Jones
ISBN: 978-0-4704-5539-5

*"Jones provides the single best introduction
to the Emergent Church movement, of which
he is a prominent leader."*
—Publishers Weekly

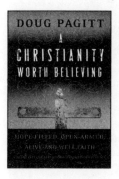

A Christianity Worth Believing
Hope-Filled, Open-Armed, Alive-and-
Well Faith for the Left Out, Left Behind,
and Let Down in Us All
Doug Pagitt
ISBN: 978-0-4704-5534-0

"A Christianity Worth Believing *is a guide
for Christians who doubt their own faith but
are not yet ready to give up on it all. Seeking
to inspire souls to find their faith once more
by addressing common problems and
answering the questions not normally
answered, [it] is a choice pick for anyone
who wants to reclaim their religion."*
—Midwest Book Review

Credits